CUSTOM KNIFEMAKING

CUSTOM
KNIFEMAKING

10 Projects from a Master Craftsman

Tim McCreight

Stackpole Books

Published by
STACKPOLE BOOKS
Cameron and Kelker Streets
P.O. Box 1831
Harrisburg, PA 17105

Printed in the U.S.A.

Library of Congress Cataloging in Publication Data

McCreight, Tim.
  Custom knifemaking.

  Bibliography: p.
  Includes index.
  1. Metal-work. 2. Knives. I. Title.
TT123.M33 1985 621.9'32 85-2844
ISBN 0-8117-2175-2

So the wind won't
blow it all away.

—Richard Brautigan

Contents

Making the Initial Weld
Restacking and Making Further Welds
Shaping Blade and Tang
Hardening and Tempering
Etching to Reveal Pattern
Bolster and Guard
Assembling the Handle

Acknowledgments

For their encouragement and support, I'd like to thank the many smiths I've talked with over the last three years as I was gathering information. I'd also like to thank the fine knifemakers who contributed photographs to this book. Their openness and enthusiasm are hard to match. Valuable technical advice on the manuscript came from Bob Griffith, Steven Crosby, and Steve Edwards. Patty Bolz and Margaret McCandless spent many hours reviewing and polishing the manuscript. The efforts of all these kind people are visible on every page. Whatever flaws remain in the manuscript are my doing, not theirs.

For constant support and good humor I especially want to thank my family, Jay, Jobie, and Jeff.

Unless otherwise noted, all photographs are by Hopkins and Hopkins, of Worcester, Massachusetts.

All drawings are by the author.

Safety Warning

PLEASE READ THIS WARNING

Knifemaking, like just about anything else you do with your hands, involves some risks. Throughout this book specific techniques include relevant precautions, but I'd like to say a general word or two right here at the beginning.

All the instructions in this book assume common sense and sober judgment on the part of the reader. Knifemaking involves sharp tools and powerful machinery; there's just no way around it. Before starting to work, mentally break each process into its component parts and examine it for potential dangers. A problem foreseen is a problem averted. This list of basic safety rules applies in all situations and is given as a reminder.

Read this page often. This is for *your* safety.

- *Never work when drowsy, preoccupied, or intoxicated.*
- *Always wear goggles when using a power grinder, sander, or drill.*
- *Never wear loose clothing when using power equipment. This includes hats and scarves.*
- *Always read labels and understand fully the ingredients and dangers of every chemical in your shop.*
- *Never startle or interrupt another worker at a power machine.*
- *If you're teaching someone, don't assume they know these safety rules. Explain them and insist on their use.*

Introduction

It is not hard to imagine that a knife was the first tool to be made by our primitive ancestors. In every corner of the globe, at every period of recorded history, every civilization has built up a rich tradition of knives. The study of blades tells anthropologists a great deal about a culture, but the interest that brings you to a book like this is probably less academic.

A knife is a direct extension of the hand and the will. Perhaps this accounts for the attraction that knives have for so many people. Knives combine beauty and utility in a wonderfully human scale. They are a practical example of the harmonizing of many elements into an object of lasting value. The history and diversity of knifemaking is vast and includes not just the camping and fighting knives that receive popular attention, but their hardworking siblings like paring knives, gardener's knives, and fancy pen knives.

Because you are reading this book, I'd guess that you already know how appealing knives can be. You might also know of the special magic that comes from making a knife. There is a rare pleasure in successfully orchestrating technical and design elements to create an object that is personally meaningful. If you've never made a knife, this book can get you started. If you've had some experience, you'll find enough diversity here to ensure some fresh ideas for your work.

This book provides practical instruction on many aspects of knifemaking. It is my intention to open this experience to a wide audience. The directions given here, seasoned with a little common sense, will allow any reader to discover the pleasure of making a knife.

Goose Wing Broad Axe, Austrian, 16th–17th century.

In many ways this book is like a cookbook. Even experienced cooks use cookbooks, but as skills increase, personal variations are introduced. I hope that readers of this book will feel free to move beyond the "recipes" given here, mixing, matching, and inventing original components in their knives. Like many cookbooks, this text gives much attention to details, opening the field to students with little background. Those readers with some experience will easily pass over these details without losing the impact of the lesson.

To cover a lot of material in an efficient way, this book is designed around a series of projects. Ten very different knives are made here, each one introducing new techniques and design challenges. Together they comprise a survey of knifemaking skills. The projects are arranged in a logical sequence, beginning with the simplest and increasing in complexity with each project. Because some readers will have had experience with knifemaking, the text is cross-referenced. In this way a reader can jump in at any point in the progression, flipping back as needed to information provided in preceding chapters.

I have started each of the projects from scratch. Each knife is an original design, cut from stock materials and worked into a knife entirely under my own hands. It's possible to buy precut parts and blades that have been ground and heat-treated. Those readers who favor this approach will be able to bypass the sections of text that do not relate to their project. If there's any point I'm trying to make, though, it is that *anyone* can make a knife from scratch. There's a great pleasure in conceiving and executing a completely original object. I hope you'll give it a try.

Each chapter begins with a brief Overview of the construction of that particular knife. For some, this will provide enough information to get started. Matters of form and function are briefly examined in a short section called Design Considerations. This is followed by a detailed description of the steps and techniques used for that project. This section is called Process Detail. Novice knifemakers are advised to start at the beginning and work through each project. Those who have an independent nature will find they can choose any project and search out the information they need.

The first five chapters are important for anyone learning to make knives. The information covered in these chapters will apply to most knives and provides a foundation on which proper knifemaking can be built. Chapter 1 deals with the tools used by the knife handcrafter. Chapter 2 describes the metallurgy of tool steels and includes a handy synopsis of steels that are popular among knifemakers. The third chapter describes the shapes of knives and presents a glimpse of their rich history. The fourth chapter describes sheathmaking and gives examples of three kinds of sheaths. Chapter 5 describes a makeshift forge and provides an introduction to blacksmithing.

Knifemaking has undergone a renaissance in the past several decades. Increased interest, education, and expanding markets have encouraged knifemakers. Several dozen full-time professional handcrafters have contributed photographs of their work to be included here to inspire your creative efforts. Their fine work indicates the high caliber of craftsmanship and the wide range of innovative design seen in knifemaking today.

Whether your interest is in making a masterpiece or a simple household tool, the best way to learn about knifemaking is to roll up your sleeves and get to work. With care and perseverance, you'll be able to share in the rich tradition and genuine rewards of knifemaking. Good luck!

1

Tools

I should say right away that I have a bias toward simple tools. The idea of buying a lot of expensive tools might discourage a person from getting started in knife-making. If I keep it simple, you may find that you already have many of the tools you'll need.

For the beginner simple tools are usually less dangerous and easier to control than more complicated ones. And because they are simple, they are easier to learn to use. You'll spend less time learning the tools and more time making knives. Because this book is not aimed at full-time production knifemakers, I won't go into detail about the equipment that is available for the manufacturer. Readers who become involved to that degree will acquire larger and more complicated tools in a natural evolution. As they do, they'll also pick up the knowledge needed to use those tools.

One more reason for preferring simple tools is the unique irregularity they give to the work they do. A typewriter, for instance, is a dandy tool but it conveys nothing of the personality that makes handwriting so interesting. The irregularities that result from using simple tools are not blunders that detract from an object. They are human marks that give it life. It is not my goal to make the same kind of knife I can buy in a hardware store. Therefore I'm not interested in investing in machines that will erase my personal gesture.

For this same reason I will not describe the use of each tool too meticulously. I hope you will develop your own ways of working. It's here, I think, that a lot of the pleasure lies.

Keep in mind, too, that there is no "right" way to equip a workshop. The following recommendations are my own.

A metal-cutting band saw is a great tool for cutting out blades. Though this is needed for a production shop, simple and less expensive equipment is suitable for the average knifemaker. (Courtesy of Rockwell International, Power Tool Division)

I offer them only as a starting place for your collection. If you talk to a dozen knifemakers you'll get a dozen different ideas about what tools you'll need. Common sense and the progress of the work will be your best guide.

CUTTING TOOLS

Let's start at the top of the line. Probably the best cutting tool for the knifemaker is a *band saw*. The correct machine will have a slow speed (about 800 feet per minute) and a heavy-duty motor. It will be fitted with a metal-cutting blade that has small teeth, probably something around 25 teeth per inch. These saws can be bought through hardware stores or tool supply companies. You can expect to pay about $350 for a new machine. Occasionally a used machine comes on the market, especially through the consolidation of small factories or schools. Many cities have dealers who specialize in used equipment. A look in the Yellow Pages can be worthwhile.

Band saws made for woodworking can be used to cut metal but the speed must be slowed down, and the blade must be changed. If the machine is not equipped with a series of pulley wheels, it is possible to rig up the necessary adjustment yourself. A good hardware store or industrial supplier can help with the materials and the know-how.

An alternative is the *hacksaw*. The principal limitation of the hacksaw (besides the fact that it runs on effort instead of electricity) is that it makes only straight cuts. A hacksaw is a handy tool to have around the house, but its shortcomings will become apparent and frustrating to a knifemaker.

Another tool that makes only straight cuts is the *cut-off wheel*. This is a thin disk of very hard material that is mounted on a motor spindle. It cuts very rapidly but will not go around corners. The cut-off wheel can be dangerous if the metal is not held perfectly straight. Because of the wheel's thinness it is fragile and can break apart violently if not properly used. In factory situations where jigs and guards are used to guide the workpiece, cut-off wheels provide a useful tool but I don't recommend them for the home workshop.

My favorite cutting tool is the *jeweler's saw*, a light tool that looks at first glance like a coping saw. It has a thumbscrew at each end of the blade and a similar screw along the back, used to adjust the blade tension. Frames are available at some hobby shops or from a jeweler's supply company (see list of suppliers at

the end of the book). In my experience, sawframes costing less than $10 are too frail and imprecise to be worthy investments. Because a sawframe will literally last a lifetime, it is worth spending the few extra dollars needed to get a good one.

Frames are sized according to the throat, or distance from the blade to the back of the frame. Something around 4 inches is a handy all-purpose size.

The sawframe is used with jeweler's sawblades. These are available from any dealer that sells frames. Their sizes are described in a number system that goes from 8/0 at the small end of the scale through 3/0, 2/0, 1/0, 0, 1, 2, 3, and so on up to 8 at the large end. Something around size 4 or 5 is appropriate for the 1/16-inch and thicker stock typical in knifemaking. For help in using the sawframe, see chapter 6.

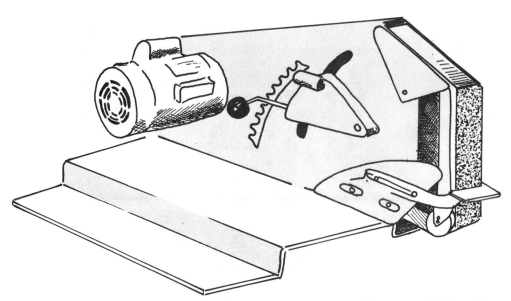

This is one of the many styles of belt sanding machines popular among knifemakers. This unit, called the Square Wheel Grinder, can be set up in many configurations.

SHAPING TOOLS

The tools listed above are used to cut out the outline or silhouette of a knife. The next job is to shape the blade and the other parts of the knife like the guard and the handle, and so on. This is really where the character of the knife is formed, so these tools are very important. Again, let's start by looking at the best tool for the job.

A *sanding machine* that drives a belt of abrasive paper is the most versatile and efficient tool for shaping a knife blade. These machines are available in several styles, the differences usually being in the width and length of the belt, the configuration of the machine, and the size of the motor. A 2 to 4-inch belt is usually preferred by knifemakers. It allows a broad enough cut to avoid carving furrows into the steel, but is small enough to be controlled. Sanding machines are designed to combine several important features. These include ease in changing belts, accessibility to the work area, and versatility of function (like having both a hard and a flexible pad against which to work). Each professional knifemaker will have his or her preference, based on individual style and work methods. The cost of a good sander starts at $500 and goes up from there. This is of course a worthwhile investment for the professional and is a reasonable price for a well-made tool. Beginners may be assured that more modest equipment is also available.

A *bench grinder* is a small motor (usu-

Bench grinders like this one can be bought at hardware and tool supply companies. Be sure to understand safety precautions before using this or any other power machine. (Courtesy of Rockwell International, Power Tool Division)

ally ¼ or ⅓ horsepower) that has grinding wheels mounted on its spindles. These wheels are thick disks of a tough abrasive, usually fused together within a ceramic material. They are available in several grades of coarseness and can be bought in many diameters. A 6-inch wheel is a popular size.

A bench grinder can be improvised from motors and attachments that fit on drills, but I do *not* recommend going about it this way. A jerry-rigged device can be dangerous. The wheel must be shrouded by a cast-iron or steel sleeve over the top and should have a small rest in front of the wheel upon which the workpiece is held. A grinding wheel should never be used without these safety precautions. Once you go to the trouble of installing them you will have spent more money than the cost of a proper bench grinder. Remember too, that safety goggles *must* always be worn while working on any power grinder or sander.

For safety, control, and low cost, the tool I prefer for shaping knives is the *file*. The ten projects in this book were shaped almost exclusively with files. It will come as no surprise, then, when I say that files are among the most important tools in the workshop.

You'll need a couple large files in a couple different shapes. That sounds like an easy order, but it quickly gets complicated.

Imported files are indexed by number, with the lower numbers representing coarser cuts. The system runs from 00, the coarsest, through whole numbers to 8, the finest. A knifemaker might want to have a 00, a 1, and a 3.

Traditional American cuts are described by names, and unfortunately the names don't give much clue about the file's cut. The coarsest category is called *bastard*. These are used for radical stock removal. Files with medium-size teeth are called *second cut*. The finest tooth size is the *smooth cut*, which gives the finest finish.

Some American manufacturers also produce a line of better-quality files that copy the European number system. These are known collectively as *Swiss Pattern Files*. These files are generally smaller than those just mentioned and are often a better-quality file. They cost more but in my opinion their cost is justified by their longer life, better control, and neater cut.

Also available are files with unusual cuts that have been developed for special uses. Several of these are particularly good at removing a lot of tough material fast. This makes them just the thing for knifemaking. Some that I have found useful are the Super Shear, the Whiscut, and the Magicut. These are available from many of the suppliers listed in the back of this book and can be tracked down through local hardware stores.

Though files are made in many shapes, you will probably need only two or three. The most commonly used shape is the flat file, a rectangular piece of steel with teeth on all sides. For maximum control, one of the narrow edges should be smooth. If the file you buy doesn't have this safe edge, make one side smooth by grinding it. If grinding, remember to quench the file in water as soon as it becomes too hot to hold. The file will lose its strength if it is heated to the point where it shows a blue color. Don't forget to dry your file well or it will rust.

Another shape you'll need is a half-round file. This has one flat side and one curved surface. Most half-round files taper to a point, so the curve offers a range of radii as the point tapers. Having a flat and a half-round file in a coarse and a medium tooth (e.g. 0 and 2, or bastard and second cut) will be a good start on a file collection.

Beyond these you might find use for a triangular, a square, and a round file.

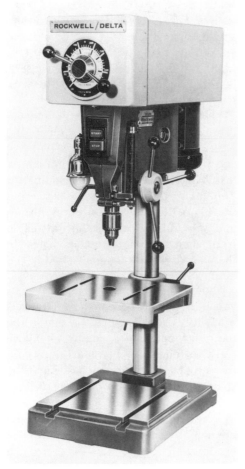

A drill press makes accurate placement of holes a simple matter. This is a bench model. They are also available as free-standing floor models. (Courtesy of Rockwell International, Power Tool Division)

The need for these and other shapes will depend on the designs you create for your knives and on your personal working style.

A file is a hard object but one of the things that will cut it is another file. Care in storing files will lengthen their life considerably. Keep the files in a divided drawer or silverware tray so they don't rub against one another. If your workshop is damp, spray the files with a rust inhibitor such as WD-40 or buy antirust paper and line the storage drawer with it. A good file is a pleasure to use and can be a surprisingly effective tool. If you buy top-quality files and take care of them, your money will go much farther than if you settle for the economy brands.

DRILLING TOOLS

It's a rare knife that doesn't have at least one hole drilled in it. To equip your workshop properly you will want at least a small set of drill bits, such as a set that runs from 1/16 to 1/4 inch (2 to 6mm) and includes about a dozen bits. Avoid buying the absolute cheapest bits. These tend to wear out very quickly.

For the tool that spins the bit, you have several choices. The top of the line in this category is the *drill press*. This is a machine that includes a motor, a vertical spindle equipped with a chuck to hold the bit, and a platform on which the work is set. Presses are sold as floor or bench models. The choice depends on your available space more than anything else. These are large pieces of equipment and can run into a lot of money. Recently, moderately priced models have appeared on the market for about $150. This makes them affordable to the serious knifemaker and they are a handy tool to own. A big advantage of the drill press is that it holds the bit perfectly vertical, guaranteeing a straight hole exactly where you want it. Because the tool is mounted, the press also frees up the user's hand and makes it easier to hold onto the workpiece.

The next best choice is a hand-held *power drill*. These look like a fat gun and are available from hardware and discount stores in a wide range of prices. I recommend getting a good model. This is a versatile tool that will see a lot of use. I advise buying an industrial-grade, variable speed drill with either a ¼-inch or ⅜-inch chuck. You can expect to pay between $25 and $40.

FINISHING TOOLS

Once the blade has been cut out and shaped, it is necessary to remove the marks made by the rough tools. This process is called finishing. Most of this work is done with abrasive papers, either by a machine or by hand.

Knifemakers equipped with the sanding machine described a few pages back can use the same machine to finish the blade. In fact, when the belt sander is used, the process of shaping flows into the finishing process without any clear dividing line between the two.

Attachments are available for electric drills that aid in the finishing process. These are wheels of various diameters that have abrasive papers either on their edges (circumference) or on the face of the disk. Many brands, sizes and configurations are made. The choice is really one of personal preference and availability. Your best bet is to pick up a vari-

ety and make your own decision about how effective each one is. The only rule that applies to all of these tools is that you *must* wear goggles when you use them.

ABRASIVE PAPERS

In any finishing operation the process is a progression from coarse to fine abrasives. Individual experience is the best guide to the specific grits preferred, but a typical selection would run from #80 through #100, #240, to #360. The paper I recommend is coated with particles of *silicon carbide*, a very hard, man-made material. This is glued onto papers and belts and is available through most hardware stores. It is sold in 9 x 11-inch sheets and in a variety of belt sizes. Some knifemakers, particularly those working on a production scale, prefer to make up their own belts and buy abrasive strips in large rolls.

A very effective tool called a *sanding stick* can be made by wrapping sandpaper around a short flat stick as shown. Any wood slat can be used. If you are going to a lumberyard, ask for lattice stripping. A piece about a foot long is used for each grade of paper. Lay strips of masking tape along the grit side of each piece, allowing about half of the tape width to hang over the edge. Set this onto the stick and scratch a line along the edge of the wood so the paper will make a crisp bend there. Roll the stick over onto the paper and score the paper again. Continue doing this until all the paper is wrapped around. Cut off any extra. This stick provides backing for the paper, which ensures a flat surface, while the wrapping makes it possible to tear off each layer as it wears out.

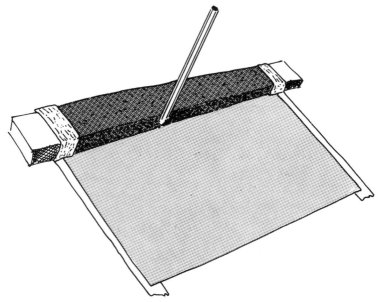

To get the best control and leverage with abrasive papers, make a sanding stick like this. Use a strip of wood about 1 foot long and 1¼ inches wide. Corners are made crisp by scoring the fold with a blunt point, as shown.

Silicon carbide paper is surprisingly tough and lasts longer than most people expect. It can clog as you use it but this can be corrected by wiping it on a rag.

Another finishing material that I've found useful around the shop is a plastic pad called *Scotch-Brite*. This is a substitute for steel wool and has the advantage of being water-resistant and free of oil. It can be bought in hardware stores, automotive supply companies, and even in the grocery store, where it is sold as a pot scrubber. Use this after abrasive papers have removed all the scratches and file marks from a piece to make a frosted finish. I also use it to clean metal before glueing and soldering.

A mirror finish can be given to metal with a *buffing stick* if fine abrasive papers have correctly prepared the surface. This

is a simple tool you can make yourself. A piece of leather is glued onto a flat stick and saturated with a polishing compound. I've found an inexpensive source for leather strips in old straps and belts bought at a flea market or thrift shop. Use epoxy to glue these onto a stick, and after the glue has set trim off any overhang with a sharp knife.

The leather can be treated with any abrasive compound. You'll find many available from hardware stores, jewelry supply companies, or automotive suppliers. A few traditional choices are Tripoli, White Diamond, Zam, Bobbing, Stainless Compound, and Crocus. These are rubbed into the leather periodically as the stick is used. Before long the leather will become saturated with the compound.

A Damascus boot knife by Don Campbell. This knife has an ivory spacer, Damascus guard and butt. The handle is of fossilized "oosik." (Photo by Gene Fletcher Brownell)

If you continue in knifemaking you'll soon be tempted to progress to a machine to help with the job of making the metal shiny. One option is to clamp the electric hand drill mentioned above into a jig as shown. For portability you might want to fasten the holder to a board that can be clamped to the workbench for use and moved around as needed. This system is faster than buffing by hand and will give an idea of the feel of power buffing, but I see it as a stopgap solution. One objection to this arrangement is that it lacks the supports and safety features of a larger machine. Also, it puts a strain on the small motor of the drill and will soon wear it out.

A better solution is called a *buffing machine*. For occasional use a simple buff can be rigged up from a common ¼ horsepower motor that runs at 1,725 RPM. This is the same motor used in most washing machines, dryers, refrigerators, and heating systems. This is to say, it's a common machine, available through equipment distributors or used, through secondhand shops.

To set up the buff it must be mounted

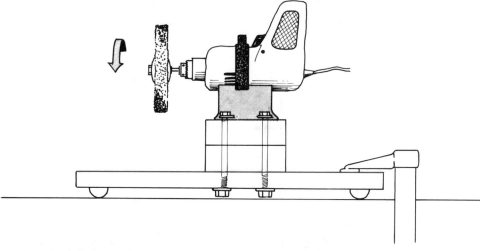

An electric drill can make an improvised buffing machine. Notice how the setup has been mounted on a board that is clamped to the workbench. This makes it possible to move the machine easily. The rig is set on rubber feet to prevent sliding on the bench and to reduce noise.

to a table or pedestal. See the drawing for details. By fixing it to a board and then clamping the board down you can allow for changing its location in the workshop. Be sure to mount the motor high enough on the table to provide clearance for the buff with at least 2 inches of free space below it.

The wheel must be arranged so the rotation is downward. Start the motor and check this direction so you can point the spindle to the left or right as needed. Many motors provide a mechanism inside the housing for reversing this direc-

tion. If one orientation suits your location better than the other, talk to an electrician for help in switching the rotation.

To outfit the motor so it will hold a buff you will need a *mandrel*. These are made in two styles. One has a threaded rod with a nut and the other is a threaded taper. The former is available through a hardware store, while the latter is best found at a jewelry supply company. The tapered spindle allows quick changing of buffs but if you foresee using only one buff, this feature is unnecessary. Which-

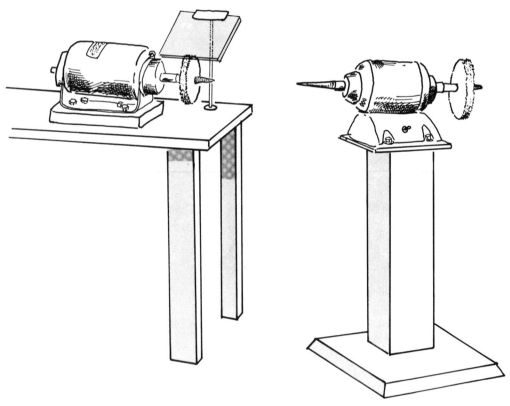

This shows two versions of buffing machines. Note the tapered, threaded mandrel on the pedestal machine. This allows for rapid changing of buffs. The benchtop model is rigged with a Plexiglas safety shield.

ever you choose, you must match the mandrel to the diameter of the motor's spindle. Be sure to measure this before you buy anything.

The wheels themselves are available in a staggering selection. You'll need a stiff muslin wheel of around 60-ply, or about ½ inch thick. This can be bought from a jewelry supply, a hardware store, or an automotive supply company. Several thin wheels can be stacked to achieve the desired thickness. Wheels are sold in both stitched and unstitched versions. I don't recommend using an unstitched wheel because it is too floppy for the heavy cutting required on steel.

When purchased, the wheels are un-treated. They must first be raked out and then coated with an abrasive com-pound before they are ready to work. To rake out the loose threads, set the buff onto the motor and put on goggles and a face mask or scarf. Turn the motor on. Hold an old fork against the wheel and you'll generate a shower of lint and small threads. Keep this up for about a minute, until the shower slows down. The wheel is then dressed by holding a bar of com-pound against it for a few seconds. Avoid the temptation of overloading the wheel. Excess will only fall off and make a mess without improving the cutting power of the buff. If the wheel clogs from excess compound during use, it can be raked in the same way. Usually raking is needed only when starting a new wheel and per-haps once a month.

The buffing wheel is a dangerous tool, the more dangerous because it looks pretty tame. Like any power tool it de-serves respect and caution. For your own safety please read these rules carefully and make a real effort to follow them every time you use the buffing machine.

Rules

1. Always wear goggles when using the buff. Always. A respirator is also a good idea and a must if you have a history of breathing problems.
2. Hold the work in a "break-away grip." Pinch the work in such a way that it can leave your hands cleanly if the wheel pulls it from your fingers. Never entwine your fingers into the work.
3. Stay alert. The machine is monoton-ous and promotes daydreaming. This is extremely hazardous! Make a con-scious effort to keep your attention focused on the work at hand. If you find your mind wandering, take a break.
4. Keep long hair and loose clothing tied back.

HAMMERS

Some metalsmiths delight in a huge collection of hammers but to get started there are only two hammers you really need. The first is a medium-size (10-ounce) *ball-peen hammer*. It will be used to flatten and straighten metal and can be used to make rivets. A better tool for this last task is a *riveting hammer*. This light-weight cross-peen hammer can be bought through a jeweler's supply com-pany. Your local hardware store will have its close equivalent under the name of an upholsterer's tack hammer. Chapter 5 describes further hammers that are used to shape red-hot metal when working with a forge but for now these two will answer your needs.

TORCHES

Throughout the projects in this book there are many references to the use of

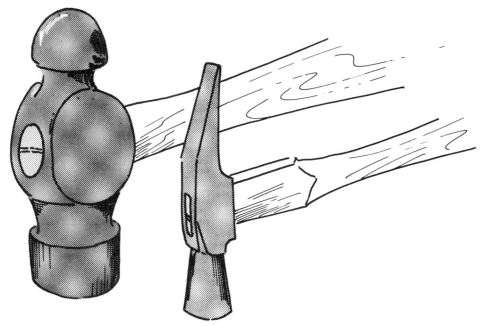

These are two of the most commonly used hammers in the shop. On the left is a ball-peen hammer. On the right is a lightweight riveting hammer.

heat. In fact without heat you can't make a good knife. There are many kinds of torches available, and each has its advantages and drawbacks. For specific advice and prices consult a local welding supply shop.

An *oxy-acetylene torch* uses two tanks of gas to produce a very hot flame. This torch supplies the broadest range of heat and flame size of all the torches listed here. It produces heat in the 5,000°F range and is the only one listed here that can cut metal. A special torch head is needed for this. These units are often sold as sets that include everything you will need except the tanks of gas, which are usually leased. For some jobs, like soft soldering, this torch has the disadvantage of being too intense.

Another choice is a single-tank unit called an *acetylene/atmosphere* or *Prestolite* torch. It uses acetylene gas mixed with atmospheric air that is drawn into the torch head through small holes in the tip. It operates in the 2,000 to 2,800°F range, so it clearly does not have the capability to heat large pieces quickly like the oxy-acetylene unit. On the other hand it is most comfortable in the temperature range used in jewelrymaking. Small tanks for this torch can be bought outright; larger tanks are leased.

Hardware and discount stores sell a *propane torch* that works off a small disposable tank. These are inexpensive and provide an excellent way for the beginner to get started without a large investment. There is little choice of flame size and the tank can be awkward to hold, but for the money this is a practical torch.

With a little cunning and some patience most of the projects in this book can be made using this torch.

Also available at discount stores is a sibling of the propane torch that uses solid pellets to provide oxygen, the necessary ingredient of a very hot flame. These have a more intense heat but are more difficult to control and usually produce a large flame.

MISCELLANEOUS TOOLS

There are many other small pieces of equipment that make up a knifemaker's workshop. Many of these will be acquired as the need for them arises. Tools that are favorites of one person might go unused in another shop. Again you'll have to make these decisions as your work progresses. Some of the miscellaneous tools I find handy are:

a heavy vise (at least 25 pounds)
a scribe
dividers (like a compass, but they have
  no pencil)
a centerpunch
wire snips (diagonal cutters)
a steel ruler
a couple pairs of Vise-Grip pliers
a couple C-clamps
assorted pieces of copper, brass, and
  nickel silver wire
scraps of leather
Band-Aids

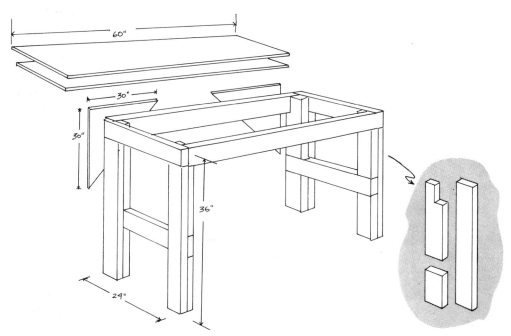

This drawing illustrates a sturdy workbench made from conventional lumberyard materials. The legs and apron are of 2 x 4s, and the top is of ½-inch plywood. The detail shows how the legs are assembled.

THE WORKSHOP

Of course the very best of all these tools won't do you much good without some place to use them. The place you work will affect the quality of your knives and the pleasure you get from making them. Time and money spent on fixing up your work space is as important as the energy you put into buying the tools that go there.

Your shop must be comfortable, a place where you want to spend time. If it is cold, damp, drafty, dark, noisy, cluttered, or cramped, you won't want to go there. Why would you? Of course we can't all sit down with an architect and design the perfect shop, but within the limits of the space you have available, take the time to lay out a workshop that will be a pleasure to use.

You'll need a heavy workbench or counter. This should be a comfortable height, probably about waist high or a little higher. The drawing shows a rugged construction that can be made for about $30 with simple equipment and standard wood from a lumberyard. Of course many other styles of bench are possible. One approach is to modify other kinds of tables. An old desk, for instance, can sometimes be found cheaply at a yard sale or used office supply company. It can be made into an excellent workbench. It should be heavy enough to stay in one place and rugged enough to stand up to the pounding of making rivets and the

Three knives by Master Shiva Ki. All are of Damascus steel and share a direct approach to design.

vibrations that come along with power equipment. It also helps if it's not too pretty. A workbench that you treat like living room furniture is probably not going to give you all the service it should. If the desk unit is too low, it can be raised on bricks or blocks of wood to bring it up to a comfortable height.

Light fixtures are as important a part of your workshop as any tool on the bench. Fluorescent fixtures are inexpensive to buy and to operate and provide a broad bright illumination. There is no reason to make do with inferior lighting. Don't settle for Grandma's old floor lamp, hung sideways and fitted with an oversize bulb. This also brings up the matter of electric cords and outlets. Use some common sense here and avoid the potential for a dangerous accident or fire. It doesn't cost much to use the right length heavy-duty extension cord. If more power is needed in your workshop area, have an electrician come in to install outlets. This can run into some money, but when set against the cost of a fire, you'll see how affordable it is to have the job done right.

If you have the luxury of space, give thought to how the shop will be laid out. Use a floor plan and pieces of paper cut to scale to play with the placement of your equipment and "furniture." A book on kitchen planning will be helpful here and will describe the basic options of a U-shape, a corridor layout, a central worktable, and so on.

Of course as you use the workshop your needs will become more evident. Take the time periodically to clean, reorganize, and upgrade your workshop. An hour spent this way will be paid back not only in a more efficient work place, but in the pleasure that comes with a well-designed space.

2

Materials

A BRIEF HISTORY

Though we think of knives as being made of steel, for most of human history other materials have been used. A survey of knife materials offers a panorama of the technological advance of mankind and a step-by-step description of man's understanding of the world.

Man's earliest tools were made of stone. In time, certain stones were found to take on a sharper edge than others. This awareness represented a technological advance. A huge advance was realized about 5,000 years ago when early man learned to control molten metal. This began a period of experimentation and discovery that has gone on uninterrupted to the present day.

Early exploration looked for new metals. Those that exist in nature in metallic form, like gold, tin, and lead, were the first to be discovered. Metals that must be refined from ores took longer to discover. It's surprising to note, for instance, that it was only about one hundred years ago that scientists learned to commercially refine aluminum, the most plentiful metal on earth.

Archaeologists tell us that copper was one of the first base metals to be put to domestic use. It was found as native crystals and pounded between rocks to give it shape. It softened when heated and became fluid when very hot.

It's easy to speculate about the mythical spill in the foundry that accidently mixed molten copper with molten tin. The result was a surprisingly tough metal called bronze. This metal so outdistanced the other materials of its day in work-

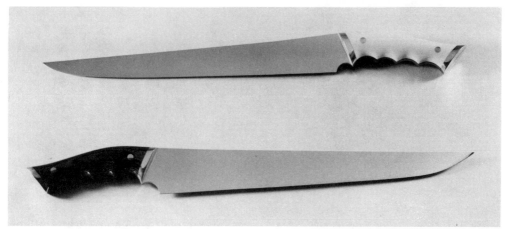

"Chef's Roast Slicer" by Joseph DiGangi. These 18-inch knives are made of ⅛-inch 440C steel. The handles are of ivory Micarta and cocobola. (Photo courtesy of the artist)

ability and strength that it gave its name to an entire age.

Eventually bronze was forced to take a position second to iron and steel. Iron first became known to the ancients in the form of meteorites. A knife from the Egyptian pyramids of 3000 B.C. is made of meteoric iron. Of course this source was limited and such objects had a mystical or ornamental value more than a practical one. The Egyptians, probably the leading scientists of their day, did not pursue steel metallurgy actively, perhaps because of the unfortunate tendency of iron to rust. They were apparently satisfied with bronze.

The Hittites were the first of the Mediterranean cultures to refine iron from ore successfully. When the Hittites attacked the Egyptians in the second century B.C., they came equipped with iron weapons. This nearly won them a victory. That would have altered the balance of power in the region and perhaps the course of history. As it was, the Egyptians used diplomacy to carry the day and learned the science of iron from their former enemies.

Within five hundred years, iron was used in virtually all the civilized world. Around 500 B.C. the Greeks invented the blast furnace and so became the world's leading supplier of iron. It is not a coincidence that this marks the beginning of Greece's Golden Age.

The strength and working properties of steel spawned a diverse technology. Equally important are the forms to which the steel was put. A survey of these would lead us through weapons to armor to architecture to civil engineering and, literally, into outer space. For all its worth, a survey like that is beyond the scope of this book. Instead we'll skip over the intervening twenty-five centuries and take a brief look at the science of steel as it stands today.

The science of metallurgy is surprisingly young. Though medieval Europe honored the trade of the blacksmith and armorer, the scientists of the day, the alchemists, were more concerned with

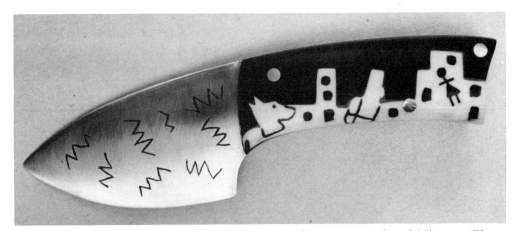

"City Knife" by David Engbritson. This 5-inch knife uses 01 steel and Micarta. (Photo courtesy of the artist)

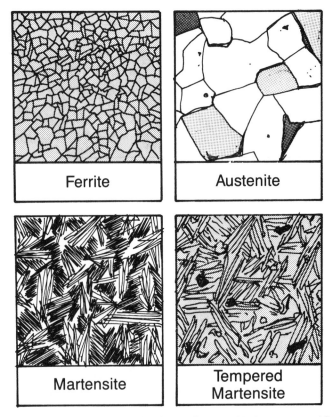

Some phases of steel as they look at about 250 times magnification.

turning base metal to gold than in understanding metals generally. It was not until 1864 that a microscope was used to study the structure of iron. Even then it took another twenty years before iron and steel manufacturers were interested enough in this research to apply its principles to the alloying of steel. With the discovery of X-ray diffraction and advances in wave mechanics in the early part of this century, metallurgy came into its own and is now a huge and vital field of study.

Each knifemaker makes decisions about what steel to use, how to shape and heat-treat it, and what qualities to expect from it. To make these choices intelligently, a basic understanding of metals is important. The following information is supplemented with tables in the Appendix.

STRUCTURE

Properties of Tool Steel

Metals, like everything else in the world, are made up of atoms. These essential building blocks, in the case of metals, are stacked together in orderly patterns called crystals. By controlling the way crystals form, grow, and organize themselves, metallurgists (and knifemakers) affect the properties of their material.

We all know that various metals have different qualities. Aluminum, for instance, is light and malleable. Lead is malleable, but very heavy. Some metals turn dark with age, others rust, and some stay shiny. These properties and many others are due in part to the chemistry of the metal (what it is made of) and in part to the shape of the crystals that make

it up. The first factor, the ingredients of a metal, are controlled by alloying. This refers to the mixing of ingredients in a metal.

By working with the second factor, the shape of the crystals and/or their arrangement within a pattern, we can alter the properties of a material. This is true of most metals, but we'll concern ourselves here with steel.

Steel is an alloy of iron and carbon. The relative amounts of these two ingredients will go a long way to determining the nature of the resulting metal. Pure iron (commercially known as *wrought iron*) is soft and brittle. The addition of carbon makes the steel tougher, up to about 0.65%, when maximum toughness is achieved. The addition of more carbon increases wear resistance, up to about 1.5% carbon. Beyond this amount, increased carbon causes brittleness and loss of malleability. Alloys containing 2 to 6.6% carbon are tough and easily melted and flow into molds nicely. They are called *cast iron*. The steels of interest to knifemakers are generally those that contain between ½ and 1½% carbon. These simple steels are known collectively as *plain carbon steel*. They are further described as low-carbon (under 0.4%), medium-carbon (0.4–0.6%), and high-carbon (0.7–1.5%).

This is a tough material, all by itself. All of the knives made in this book use a heat treatment to increase the steel's hardness. It's worth noting, though, that for a large part of recorded history a blade of untreated carbon steel would have been superior to what was commonly used.

The proper choice and use of steels is a complex matter. Keep in mind that since each of these many factors affects

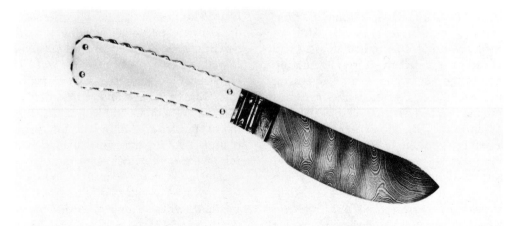

Twisted Damascus Skinner by Barry L. Davis. The blade of this knife has 384 layers. The bolsters are of nickel silver Damascus and the handle is ivory. (Photo courtesy of the artist)

the others, proper understanding of steel requires an intuitive balance of ingredients, treatments, and requirements.

Hardening and Tempering

In its soft state (that is, at its most malleable), steel exists in a form called *ferrite*. This is a solid solution made up of body-centered cubic crystals. Carbon atoms are located in the spaces between iron atoms. When this steel is heated to high temperatures, the carbides dissolve into the iron to make a structure called *austenite*. This compound is characterized by crystals having a face-centered cubic structure. The temperature at which this transformation takes place is called the *critical temperature.*

If allowed to cool very slowly (i.e. annealed), austenite will revert back to a mixture of iron and iron-carbide. It will be malleable again. If, however, the steel is cooled rapidly, the austenite forms a very hard, needlelike structure called *martensite.*

Martensite is what makes steel hard. The more martensite there is, the harder the steel will be. The amount of carbon in an alloy, the temperature to which it was heated, and the rate of the cooling will all affect how much martensite is produced.

The "needles" of martensite have carbon atoms trapped in the crystals during quenching. This strains the crystals and creates a brittle structure. An analogy would be a balloon inflated almost to the breaking point. It is under so much pressure that it is, in a sense, unstable or ready to break. To make a good knife, some of this tension (hardness) must be transformed into flexibility. This is done in a second heating operation, called *tempering.*

As the steel is reheated, the hard carbide needles dissolve into the structure. The resulting metal surrounds the hard needles of martensite in a relatively flexible matrix. The amount of dissolving determines how much hardness is sacrificed. This is a factor of temperature and time. Just about all steels and all heat treatments involve trade-offs, compromises where a theoretical ideal is replaced by a balance between conflicting factors. It's time now to translate some of these trade-offs into practical knife-making terms.

Hardness—This refers to the ability to resist penetration. It can be measured most easily by rubbing one material against another. A rock hound, for instance, rubs a specimen against a known sample to determine its hardness. The harder material will scratch the softer one and resist being scratched by it. In the mineral world, a system of numbers called the *Moh's Scale* ranks a series of ten minerals from soft to hard. Consult the Appendix for an expanded version of the Moh's Scale.

A more scientific method uses a machine that has a controlled thrust to press against a sample in such a manner that the resistance can be accurately measured. Of the several types of machine available, the most popular is called the *Rockwell Hardness Tester*. It measures the displacement response of a material to a given load and can be fitted with either a hardened steel ball or a diamond tip. The former is read on what is known as the B-scale and the latter, more common in metallurgy, is read on the *C-scale*. This series of numbers runs from 20 to 68. Note that these numbers relate only to relative penetration at a given load, rendered in terms of stress, e.g. pounds per square inch. These readings have meaning only in relation to other samples. A typical knife blade would fall between 57 and 64 and would be written, for instance, as Rockwell C-59, RC-59, or 59HRC.

Toughness—This term describes the ability of a steel to resist breaking. It is a near-opposite of brittleness.

Wear Resistance—This property is what gives a knife blade edge-holding power. It is the ability to stand up to abrasion. All tool steels are good on this, but some are better than others. See the Appendix for specifications.

Resistance to Deformation—The rapid cooling of the hardening process can cause some steels to warp or even break. This term refers to the ability of a steel to stand up to rapid changes in temperature. This property would only affect a

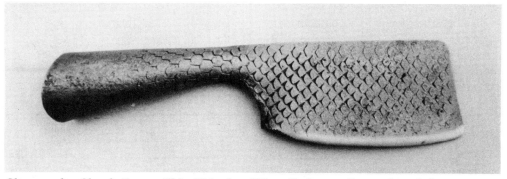

Chopper by Chuck Evans. This 10-inch self-handled utensil was forged from a rasp. (Photo courtesy of the artist)

large knife and would be most critical when the blade has cross-sections of widely varying thickness.

Depth of Hardening—As described below, hardening is achieved by rapid cooling of steel. Some alloys are able to throw off heat faster than others, meaning that thick sections can be rapidly cooled and therefore hardened. Steels with shallow hardening properties would not lend themselves to large objects that must be hardened. For most knifemakers this is not an important consideration in choosing a steel.

Machinability—This refers to the ability of a steel to cut freely and/or to leave a good finish after being machined. It is not a major concern for the hand knifemaker.

The first three properties, hardness, toughness, and wear resistance, are the factors of greatest concern to knifemakers. It is possible to buy a steel that has excellent qualities in any one of these categories. The problem is in finding a material that offers the correct balance among them all. In my opinion any of the steels listed in this chapter can be used to make an excellent knife.

As explained above, the amount of carbon in a steel has a lot to do with the nature of the metal and how it can be altered by heat treatment. Over the years, the carbon has had to make room for

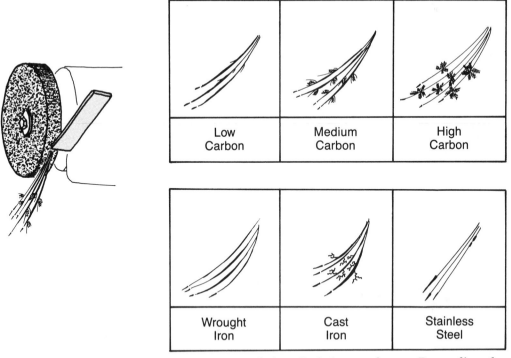

A simple way to distinguish between steels is called the spark test. By reading the spray of sparks created in grinding, a trained eye can make an educated guess about the ingredients of a steel.

other ingredients. These have been developed by modern research to achieve specific qualities in an alloy. Here is a sample of common ingredients:

Chromium—This element increases the hardness penetration, but its greatest contribution is in increased wear and corrosion resistance. Amounts of over 5% are needed before either of these qualities is significantly affected. Steels known as "stainless" have as much as 14% chromium.

Nickel—This addition adds to wear resistance and toughness, and also extends hardenability.

Vanadium—This element allows the steel to stand up to high temperatures and in use, helps to retard the growth of grain size during hardening. It also forms hard carbides, which add to its wear resistance.

Manganese—This expands the range of critical quenching, the "hardening window," making it easier to treat all areas of an object. This is especially important for large objects where a plain carbon steel would cool too slowly on the inside to be hardened.

Knowing what goes into a steel doesn't complete the picture. We need to know how much of each ingredient goes in and what the resulting alloy is called.

The American Iron and Steel Institute (AISI) and the Society of Automotive Engineers (SAE) have cooperatively devised a system that groups tool steels

Table 2.1
CLASSIFICATION OF TOOL STEELS
This chart shows a few of the steels popular among knifemakers.
Those that appear in bold type are described in the text.

% of elements

Type	Carbon	Manganese	Silicon	Chromium	Nickel	Vanadium	Tungsten	Molybdenum
W2	**0.6–1.4**					**0.25**		
W3	1.00					0.50		
W4	0.6–1.4				0.25			
S1	0.50			1.50			2.50	
S2	0.50		1.00					0.50
S3	0.50			0.75			1.00	
01	**0.90**	**1.00**		**0.50**			**0.50**	
02	0.90	1.60						
06	1.45	1.00	1.25					0.25
A2	1.00	0.60		5.25		0.25		1.00
A4	1.00	2.00		1.00				1.00
D1	1.00			12.00				1.00
D2	**1.50**			**12.00**				**1.00**
D3	2.25			12.00				
L1	1.00		1.25					
L2	0.5–1.10		1.00			0.20		
L6	**0.70**			**0.75**	**1.50**			**0.25**
L7	1.00	0.35		1.40				0.40
440C	**0.95–1.20**	**1.00**	**1.00**	**16.00–18.00**				**0.75**
154CM	**1.05**	**0.60**	**0.25**	**14.00**				**4.00**

according to their uses. Those marked in bold type are the most popular steels among knifemakers.

There is still one other factor that plays a part in the nature of steel. This is the *grain size*. Crystals group themselves into more or less orderly bundles called grains. A structure made of large grains has relatively little contact area between grains. Such a structure is brittle. Smaller grains create more *grain boundaries* and produce a structure that is denser and tougher.

Two samples having identical quantities of the same ingredients can behave differently because of the size and shape of their grains. It might help to visualize two stone walls, one made of small round stones and the other made of large irregular boulders. Even if the stones are of the same mineral and if the same mortar is used in both walls, the properties of the walls will be different.

Grains are formed when the crystals within a metal have a chance to move. This takes place at elevated temperatures. High temperatures for prolonged periods foster the greatest opportunity for migration and organization of crystals. When a sample of steel is held at a high temperature for several minutes, there is enough time for many crystals to grow into large clusters, or grains. For this reason it is inadvisable to sustain a blade at a high temperature any longer than necessary. What is "high" depends on the alloy and melting point of the steel.

A blacksmith's method of annealing (softening) hardened steel is to bring it to a red heat and allow it to cool slowly. This will achieve the softer state, but it leaves the grains very large since they have had time during the slow cool to reorient themselves into large clusters. The black-

smith will usually compensate for this by forging the steel to break up the large grains. An accomplished bladesmith can orient the boundary flow lines to coordinate with the shape of the blade. This will improve it. This is the argument behind those bladesmiths who maintain that a forged blade is intrinsically better than a blade made through stock removal. Given that piece of steel, the one that was annealed by slow cooling, their argument is right.

Through careful heat treatments it is possible to anneal steel without causing the formation of large grains. This is called *normalizing*. To normalize steel, it is heated to about 100°F above its critical temperature and allowed to air-cool to room temperature. Normalized steel has a fine grain structure and can be made into knives that are every bit as strong as forged blades.

A factor far removed from the science of steel, but every bit as important, is availability. All the steel mentioned here can be bought commercially, but some alloys are easier to procure than others. Knifemakers working in a large volume will want to take the time to track down sources and will be in a position to order the large quantities often required by suppliers. For such knifemakers I recommend phone calls to local distributors and sheet-metal fabricators. Check the Yellow Pages for possible leads.

Those just getting started in knifemaking will have different needs. At the back of this book is a list of several suppliers who sell popular knife steels in small quantities.

Many of the projects in this book have been made with an oil-hardening steel called 01. This familiar standard is an all-purpose steel, well-suited to large and

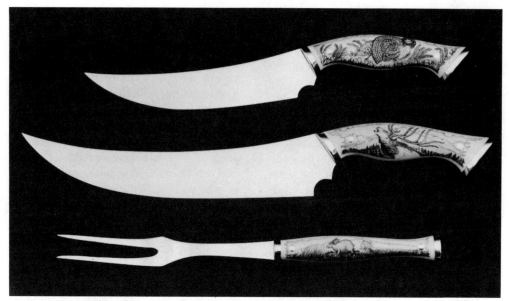

A 3-piece carving set in 440C by Joseph DiGangi. The handles are of ivory Micarta with scrimshaw by Jake Bell. (Photo courtesy of the artist)

small knives and springs in pocket knives. It is available from industrial suppliers in a form called *precision ground flat stock*. This is sold in 18-inch strips, from ½ to 6 inches wide, and from ¹⁄₁₆ to ¼ inch thick. Many suppliers stock both an oil- and an air-hardening steel. I recommend the oil-hardening as the easier material to use.

The following list starts with this steel and describes in simple terms some of the popular steels being used by knife-makers.

DESCRIPTIONS OF POPULAR STEELS

01

As shown on the chart, this steel contains about 1% carbon, which accounts for its relatively high wear resistance.

The inclusion of chromium and tungsten allows the steel to be oil-quenched, making it more stable and less likely to distort than a water-quenched material.

Heat treatment of this steel is described in chapter 6.

W2

This is a popular water-quenching steel characterized by its toughness. Because of the shock of a radical cooling (in water or brine), knives with a great variance in thickness run the risk of warpage and possible breaking.

L6

Because of the nickel in this alloy, the hardened and tempered steel is tough and very resistant to wear. It is used in the manufacture of saw blades and can be salvaged from those sources by the enterprising knifemaker. Nowadays only commercial grades of woodcutting saws are likely to contain nickel.

D2

The high chromium content of this steel contributes to its stain resistance and increases its hardness through the presence of chromium carbides. This alloy has about the greatest wear resistance of the common tool steels.

440C

This stain-resistant steel is popularly used for commercial paring knives and pocket knives. This alloy does not provide great toughness or wear resistance but it is a serviceable grade for light use.

154CM

This alloy is similar to 440C but has replaced 4% of the chromium with molybdenum. The result is a corrosion-resistant steel with great toughness and good edge-holding power. It is not the cheapest steel you can buy, nor is it the easiest to work and heat treat, but for the serious knifemaker this is probably the top-of-the-line alloy commonly in use.

OTHER KNIFEMAKING MATERIALS

Brass

All of the projects described here use brass in one way or another. Though it is familiar from everyday contact, it deserves a technical description. Brass is an alloy of copper and zinc. Alloys containing more than 30% zinc, called high-zinc brasses, are pale and very tough. They are used in machine parts and valves and are not recommended for handcrafting because they are difficult to work.

Low-zinc brasses, those having 30% zinc or less, are a bright yellow color, are generally resistant to severe corrosion, and can be easily worked. As the amount of zinc in the alloy decreases, the color becomes richer and more golden, and the metal becomes increasingly malleable. Brass is a good choice for knife fittings because it is inexpensive, durable, and attractive. It has the advantage of being worked with the same tools and finishing materials as steel. Brass is sold under several names that should be clarified.

Probably the most common alloy is the mixture mentioned above as the dividing line between the two families of brass, the mix of 30% zinc and 70% copper. This alloy is called yellow brass, 30/70 brass, cartridge brass, and Copper Development Association (CDA) #260. Its melting point is 1,749°F (954°C). Remember, all of these are the same metal.

Another popular alloy that is slightly more malleable and shows a rich golden color is called variously Nu-Gold, Jewelry Bronze, and CDA #226. It contains about 12% zinc and 88% copper. Its melting point is 1,886°F (1,030°C).

Another metal frequently used in knife fittings is called nickel silver, or German silver. These are particularly misleading names since the alloy contains no silver. This tough gray-colored metal is an alloy of copper, zinc, and nickel. It is the metal of which the 5-cent coin is made. A more accurate and useful name for the alloy is white brass, since it is really a brass with a whitener. It shares many working properties with brass, costs about the same, and melts at about the same temperature, 2,030°F (1,110°C).

Two other materials that are often used in knifemaking deserve quick mention. Micarta is a patented resin that is popular for handles. It is available plain and also in a form called linen Micarta. This is made of sheets of linen fabric impregnated with the plastic resin. It reveals a layered configuration that resembles wood grain. Linen Micarta is used in this book in the lockback folding knife made in chapter 14.

A similar material is called Pakkawood or Dymondwood. These products are made by forcibly impregnating plastic resins into natural wood. The result is a very durable wood-grained material that can be polished to a high shine. This is popularly used for handles in kitchen cutlery.

3

Knife Design

NOMENCLATURE

The drawing opposite shows two familiar knife forms with their various parts labeled. Some of these, like the blade, edge, handle, and point, are obvious, but some of the less-common terms deserve brief explanation.

Let's start with the shape of the blade. One style, in which the point curves away from the edge, is called *upswept*. The blade shape in which the spine curves downward toward the edge is called a *drop point*. Some blades, like the example shown on the left in the illustration, have a concave curve near the tip as if the blade had been clipped off there. This is called a *clip-point*. If the smaller edge is sharpened it is called a *swedge*; if unsharpened it is called a *false-edge*.

The thickest part of a blade is called the *spine*. In a single-edged blade this is along the side opposite the cutting edge. In a double-edged blade like a dagger, this is along the center of the blade. Sometimes the blade is strengthened by a trough formed into the blade near the spine. This is called a *fuller*.

The short, unsharpened area that separates the cutting edge from the handle is called the *ricasso*. If the ricasso is curved slightly to accommodate a finger grip, this section is called a *choil*. The purpose of the ricasso is to strengthen the knife in this area, which is potentially the weakest. It has the added advantage of making sharpening easier.

In many knives the handle is reinforced at the place where it meets the blade. This reinforcement is called a *bolster* and is generally made of metal. Bolsters con-

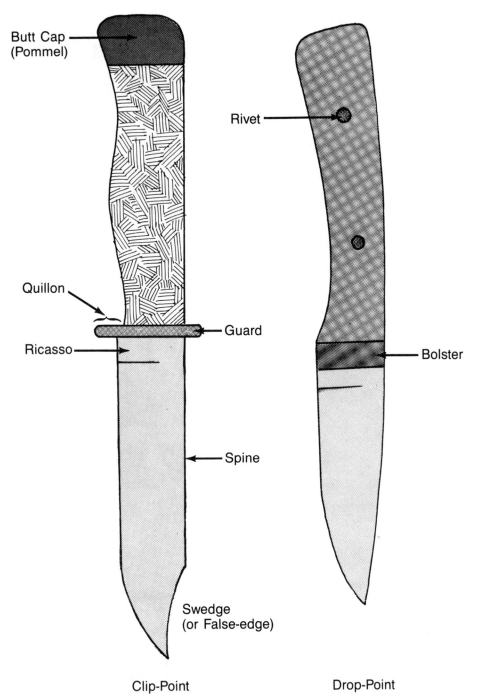

Butt Cap
(Pommel)

Quillon

Ricasso

Guard

Spine

Rivet

Bolster

Swedge
(or False-edge)

Clip-Point

Drop-Point

Some common parts of a knife.

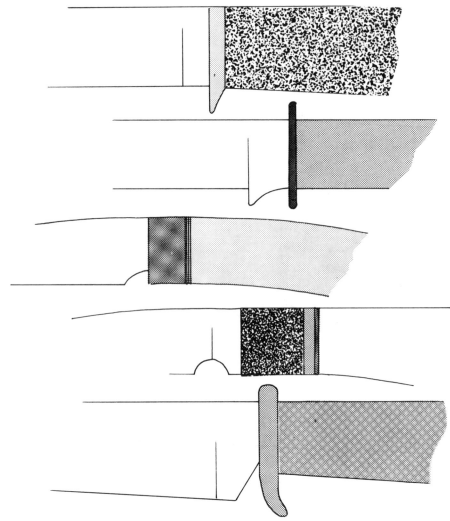

Here are a few of the hundreds of possible ways of designing the area where the blade meets the handle. This unsharpened area is called the ricasso.

form to the shape of the knife, as in the right-hand example in the drawing. Some knives include a *guard* at this point. This is a flange of metal that extends outward from the knife and serves to protect the user's hand. The projection is called a *quillon*. Some knives have a double quillon, a guard that reaches out from both the spine and the edge, and others like this example have only a single quillon.

The end of the handle is called the *butt*. It can be left plain, have a small *butt cap*, or have a large bulb of metal called a *pommel*. The purpose of this is for strength and to add weight for balance. This is especially necessary in the case of a large or long blade.

Pieces of a knife might be held in place

by *pins* or *rivets*. A pin is a rod that is cemented into place. A rivet differs in that it has a head or flared-out bulge at each end. This makes it the more secure fastener of the two. Either of these can be made to protrude or to be flush with the surface.

BLADE CROSS-SECTIONS

Imagine cutting a blade in half and looking at the end that was cut. This is called the *cross-section*, sometimes shortened to section. In determining the de-sired blade section it is important to understand the factors that go into the decision. Assuming a good-quality steel and proper heat-treating, sharpness and thinness are synonymous. Of course it is also true that a thin blade is weaker than a thick one. Some familiar examples make the choices clear. Think of the sharpest blades you have around the house. They would be razors and utility knives. Both are very thin. Now think of the strongest blades you've seen, perhaps a splitting maul or a cold chisel. Both are relatively dull. Even if the chisel is made of fine

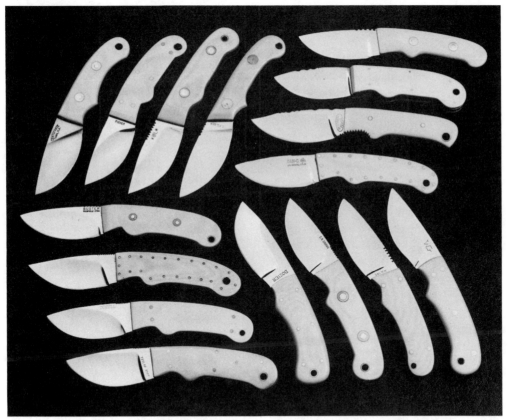

This collection of knives, commissioned by John Stahl, illustrates the many variations possible on a single style. Each of these examples has been made by a professional knifemaker, each adding his personal touch to the same basic design.

Decorative filework on the knives from John Stahl's collection.

steel properly hardened, even if you sharpen it with great care, you'll never be able to peel a carrot with it. The bevel is just too broad. This trade-off between sharpness and strength is the central issue in determining blade shapes.

The illustration shows some of the typical cross-section shapes for blades. The first example, the *flat V*, is a hard-to-beat standard shape. It provides a balance between strength and keenness. It is, coincidentally, probably the easiest blade to make by hand. After years of sharpening, as the width of the blade wears away, the knife never gets so thick that it cannot be stoned down to a keen edge.

The next example, a variation on the first, retains more thickness for greater strength. This style will give a keen edge when new but when worn down it reveals a broad edge that will be difficult to sharpen well.

The next example is called *hollow-ground*. This does not designate a hollow knife. Rather, the blade has a concave area, a section that has been "hollowed out." This is a popular commercial edge because it provides a lot of material along the spine for strength while leaving a thin edge. The extreme example of this cut is the old-fashioned straight razor. Making this shape requires a sanding machine or skilled forging. Those workers with access to the right equipment will soon learn how to stroke the blade across the abrasive belt to cut a hollow-ground edge. It can be a frustrating process to learn because the edge being cut is out of sight underneath the blade as you work. Within a few tries you'll get into the rhythm.

The next example shows a rounded blade bevel called a *convex edge*. This is the opposite of the concave and has the opposite effect. That is, it favors strength over keenness. This cross-section is used in the Wilderness Knife made in Project 5, where strength was needed more than keenness.

Next to this is a *fullered* blade. The process of fullering gets into advanced blacksmithing and is beyond the scope of this book. At red heat the blade is pinched between two rounded dies that press a trough into the knife. This adds strength while economizing on weight.

The final example shows a traditional dagger shape. The spine runs down the middle and the edges can use any of the blade configurations just listed.

KNIFE FORMAT

Having discussed the blade shape, it's time to describe the rest of the knife, the tang. I have used the larger term, *format*, here to avoid giving the impression that we first choose a blade, then choose a tang, and stick the two together. The choice of a tang depends on the subtle relationships between the shape and size of the blade, the intended use of the knife, the material of the handle, and the skills and equipment available. It's all of this together that I'm calling format. Keep in mind when choosing a tang style that it must coordinate with the rest of the knife in all these respects.

An accompanying drawing shows some popular tang styles. The first, illustrated in the first two projects, is probably the easiest and most popular. It is called a *full tang* and provides great strength.

The second, illustrated in Project 3, is

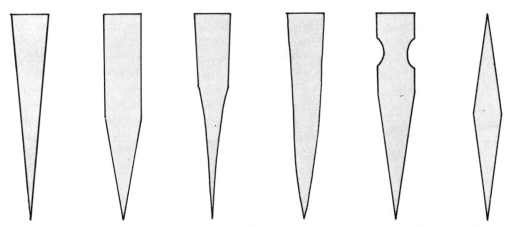

Some popular cross-section shapes for knife blades. From left to right they are: flat V, shallow V, hollow-ground, convex, fullered, and double-edged (dagger).

Four knives by Master Shiva Ki, illustrating a few knife formats. The blade material here is Damascus, or pattern-welded steel.

a *partial tang*. It is fitted into the handle and held there by a pin. In the method shown here the tang is completely enclosed within the handle. A popular style for inexpensive kitchen cutlery uses a partial tang that is exposed along the top and bottom of the handle.

The next illustration, a *through-tang*, is used in Projects 4, 6, and 10. It uses a threaded nut to tighten the handle pieces onto a thin tang that extends through the handle and out the end.

Of course, many variations are possible on each of these techniques. One of the pleasures of knifemaking is the engineering aspect of harmonizing function with materials and good looks.

CARE AND MAINTENANCE

Objects of value are worth taking care of. Most tools need periodic restoration.

For both these reasons, knives deserve a special kind of on-going attention. Because we're talking about sharp, pointed instruments, it does not seem amiss to speak of caution. Some of this might sound simplistic but there is no harm in being cautious.

Keep knives away from children. This includes a constant awareness of where you keep knives so you'll know if they present a potential danger. Of course you have knives in a drawer in the kitchen. Of course you wouldn't let a young child near them. But how about the basement workshop, the car trunk, or that box of gardening equipment? Keep *all* knives away from young kids.

Take the time to teach children proper safety rules for knives. As a reader of this book you enjoy cutlery. It is shortsighted to deny this pleasure to young people, and potentially dangerous too.

We all know how tempting forbidden fruit can be. Show the young people in your life how to use knives safely, remind them not to walk with a knife, not to whittle toward themselves and so on. Provide guidance until the child has acquired good habits as a matter of course. Everyone involved will find it time well spent.

A knife will offer a pretty clear reflection of the care given to it. If you toss it into a tool box and allow it to rattle against hammers and files, it will get dull. What else would you expect? If you keep the blade sharpened, away from moisture, protected in a sheath, and safe from abusive wear it will hold up well. It's as simple as that. Of course not all knives need to be works of art. There's nothing wrong with having an old workhorse in the tool box. The point is just that you should treat an expensive knife

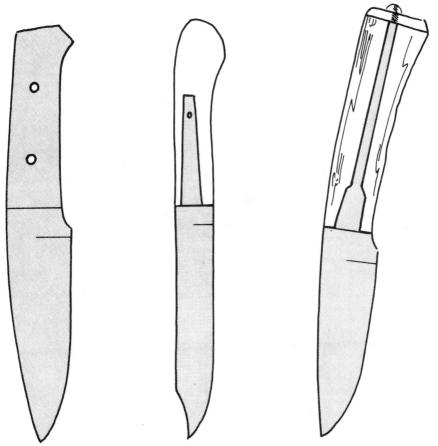

Common tang styles, all described in the project chapters that follow. These are the full-tang, the partial-tang, and the through-tang.

to a better life and in turn you can expect more from it, both in looks and in use.

SHARPENING

The keenness of an edge depends on the quality of three things: the steel, the heat treating, and the honing. Steel was discussed in the last chapter, and heat-treating techniques are discussed throughout the projects. That leaves sharpening.

The best place to start is with an understanding of what is intended. As discussed above, the blade consists of a large bevel. The cutting edge is formed by a second, much smaller bevel. This is formed on an oilstone, smoothed on a finer stone, and finally shaped on a strop.

The basic tool of sharpening is a *whetstone*. These are made of either natural quarried stone or a man-made composition. The latter, often called *India Stones*, are cheaper and will create a fine edge. Avoid the cheapest versions, and while you're at it, spring for a stone that is large enough to simplify the task, say 6 inches long. These are popularly sold in a two-sided version that has both a coarse and a fine face. They are available from a hardware store and should cost under $10. A less common synthetic stone is bright red in color and is called a *ruby* stone. It is very hard and will refine

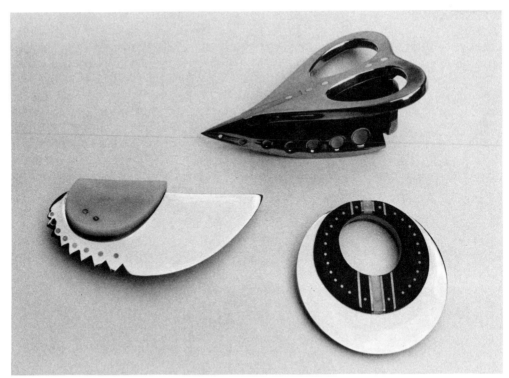

"Bitty Blades #1, #2, #3" by Michael Croft. These small and unusual knives are made of 01 steel, delrin, brass, and wood. (Photo courtesy of the artist)

a sharp edge but is too hard for a general-purpose stone.

Of the several natural stones available, the most popular is called an *Arkansas* stone. Guess where it comes from. They are used after preliminary sharpening on an India stone and give a great edge and a bright finish. These are expensive, $30 for a medium-size stone, and are in my opinion not necessary for average knife use. Because the Arkansas stone is so fine, it cannot be used to reshape a nicked blade.

Another name for a whetstone is an oilstone. This comes from the fact that the stone must be saturated with oil to get best results. It used to be that a new stone had to be soaked in a pan of oil until the pores filled up. Nowadays most stones are sold as "oil-soaked," so you are saved the bother.

Always use a light oil when rubbing steel on a sharpening stone. This lubricates the sharpening action and floats away the particles of steel as they are scraped off. Any light oil can be used (3-in-1, sewing machine oil, Marvel Mystery, etc.). Some people prefer a mixture of equal parts of a thin grade of motor oil and kerosene. Keep such a mixture in a metal can, away from any heat source. Clean your sharpening area regularly and avoid accumulating oily rags.

The synthetics and the natural stones just described are very hard. An alternative that comes from the Orient is called a *water stone*. These natural stones are quite soft and must be soaked with water all the time, even when not in use. They wear down quickly during sharpening and must be rubbed on a flat surface periodically to restore the flatness of the face. They leave a highly polished, razor-sharp edge but I don't recommend them

A 20-degree angle. This is a good average angle for sharpening. Your needs and the shape of the blade might require a slightly steeper or shallower angle.

for the casual knife user because they are time-consuming to prepare and maintain.

Start learning how to sharpen by picturing an angle of 20 degrees. The illustration will help. A bevel of this angle will yield a sharp all-purpose edge. For tools that foresee a more rugged use, increase the angle by up to 5 degrees. For sharper, more delicate knives, decrease the angle by 3 or 4 degrees. A simple method to teach yourself the proper angle is to cut a small wedge of cardboard to those angles and use it to gauge the tilt of the blade on the stone. It is impractical to hold the wedge in place when sharpening, but by keeping it close at hand and checking frequently, you can modify your guesswork and soon establish a feel for the correct angle.

Secure the stone to the workbench. Proper honing involves a good deal of pressure. If the stone is sliding away as you work, your effectiveness is greatly hampered. Set the stone in a vise, cushioned with strips of leather or soft wood, or clamp it to the bench.

An alternate method is to hold the knife stationary and slide the stone along it. This is especially recommended for small stones. If you try this method, don't hold

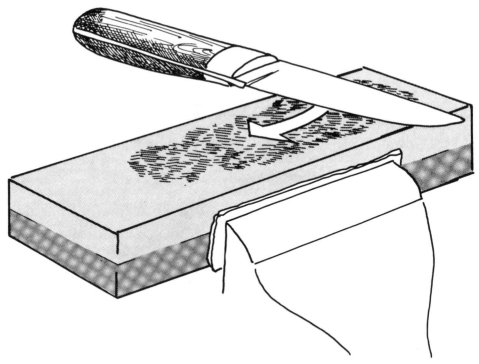

An oilstone set into a vise and ready for sharpening. Note that the vise jaws have been cushioned with leather. In sharpening, pretend you are shaving a thin layer off the top of the stone.

the knife in a vise. It should not be vertical, but at about a 45-degree angle.

Make up your mind that you'll get your hands dirty when sharpening a knife. Keep a rag or paper towel close at hand and set to work. Squirt a few drops of oil onto the stone and rub them around. Unless you've got huge nicks in the blade, start with the fine side of a combination stone. If this doesn't seem to create any changes after a full minute of rubbing, flip the stone over and work on the coarser side.

Each person has his or her own method of working. You should experiment to find the stance that is most comfortable for you. To start with, try this method and modify it until it works. Slide the blade as if you were shaving off a thin layer of the stone. Make two or three identical passes, then flip the knife over and do the same on the other side of the blade. Carefully wipe off the oil and examine the edge closely under a bright light. Use magnification if possible. You'll be surprised at how clearly you can see what's going on.

You should see a freshly cut, tiny bevel along the edge. This surface will be bright and shiny and should show a pattern of very fine lines. Those lines, the scratches from the stone, will be smoothed away in the final stropping. At this stage the most important thing to look for is an evenness in the width and angle of the bevel.

Resume cutting, either continuing the same stroke if all was in order or modifying it as needed. Check again and continue working until the edge is symmetrical.

You'll find that the point involves a little more difficulty than the body of the blade. As the stroke moves up toward the point you will have to raise and slightly pivot the knife to maintain a consistent angle along the edge. This is more complicated to describe than it is to perform. Your best bet is to practice and analyze the results.

Cutting on a stone, even a fine stone, leaves a microscopic burr on the edge. If the edge feels sharp at this stage, it is this jagged edge that feels sharp. This edge will quickly break off and leave an inferior edge. The burr must be removed to achieve a finely honed knife. This can be done in at least four ways.

The first is to chop with the knife into a block of wood and draw the blade along its edge. This will break off the burr. The second is to do the same thing in a cake of lead. This breaks and somewhat burnishes the edge. The third method is to use a machine-powered muslin buffing wheel to chip the burrs off and polish the edge. Use a hard muslin buff at a high speed. The buff should be coated with a polishing abrasive such as tripoli, white diamond, Zam, rouge, or emery. The fourth choice is to strop the blade on a piece of leather treated with the

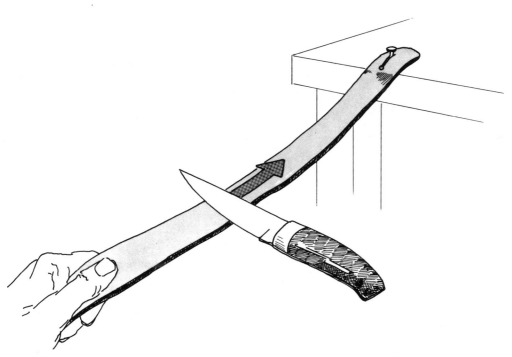

In stropping, the knife is moved away from the blade edge. This is the opposite of the sharpening stroke.

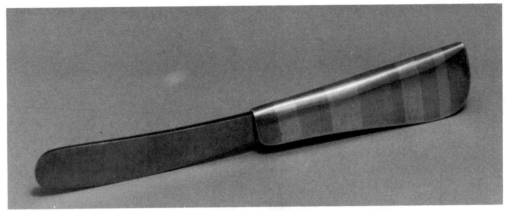

A butter knife by Janet Hessel. This 6½-inch knife is made of high carbon steel, sterling, copper, and bronze. (Photo courtesy of the artist)

abrasives just mentioned. Use the smooth side of an old belt or handbag strap. This can be attached to the bench as shown or glued to a board about a foot long and a couple inches wide. In either use, the blade is drawn backwards along the leather while held at a relatively steep angle as shown.

The resulting edge will shave the soft hairs off your arm. A more practical test is to cut a piece of leather or rope. The longevity of this edge has to do with the quality of the steel and its heat-treating, the thickness of the blade at the edge, and the use to which it is put. Keep in mind, though, that any blade will need to be resharpened once in a while. Plan on this and take the time to do it right. You will develop the skills to do the job efficiently, and along the way you'll also develop an appreciation for a keen edge.

4

Sheathmaking

No book on knifemaking would be complete without a chapter on sheaths. The preceding chapters have emphasized the toollike qualities of a knife. Decisions about materials, size, and shape are all made according to the function of the knife, the uses to which it will be put. In this way it is in the same class as a hammer or a wrench. One aspect of this toollike character is access, or the quality of being where needed when needed. To be practical, a fixed-blade knife must have a sheath. The only exception I can think of is a kitchen knife.

The requirements of a sheath are pretty straightforward. It should fit the knife, both literally and aesthetically. It should be of a durable material that is well suited to the environment in which it is expected to perform. And it should hold the knife tightly enough to prevent its

loss, but in such a way that it can be comfortably withdrawn when needed.

Leather is commonly used for sheaths and is the material we'll be working with in this chapter. Leatherwork is a serious art form that offers rich potential for craftspeople. Though in this book we can only begin to explore this interesting field, perhaps this will open a door for experimentation and further study.

The following pages show the steps used to make three basic knife sheaths. Bear in mind as you read that variations on these designs are limitless. By reading the instructions and trying a few simple projects you will soon become acquainted with the tools and materials of sheathmaking. From there your sheathmaking can develop in tandem with your knifemaking.

In these examples all the stitching was

done by hand. Leather can also be sewn on heavy-duty machines. If you are making a large number of sheaths you might investigate buying a machine. To try one out, or to have a sheath machine sewn, contact a shoemaker or leather crafter.

MATERIALS

For small users the most convenient source of leather is a local leather crafter or a leather supply store like Tandy. Besides the convenience of buying your materials from a local craft shop, there is the asset of the advice that can be found there. The variety of available leathers is overwhelming, so don't be afraid to ask for help. If you take your knifemaking into a larger scale, you will want to investigate wholesale suppliers. You can expect a minimum order restriction, but if you are in business you'll make use of a large quantity.

The most popular leather for sheaths is undoubtedly *cowhide*. Cowhide has the advantage of relatively low cost for its great durability. The sheaths made here use cowhide, and I will confine my description to that material, but you should be aware of other possibilities. There are many leathers available and after a few simple sheaths you may want to explore these. Canvas, wood, and plastic fabrics also present possibilities for an inventive sheathmaker.

The thickness of leather is described in *ounces*. This refers to the probable weight of a square-foot sample. A square foot of leather about 3/16 inch thick would weigh in at about 8 ounces. It is called 8-ounce leather and is a good weight for an average-size sheath.

In choosing your leather you will be asked not only what animal leather you want (cow) and how thick the skin should be (6- to 8-ounce), but also what tanning you prefer. The three most common systems used to tan or preserve animal skins are *chrome*, *oil*, and *vegetable*. The first uses chromium salts and the second uses

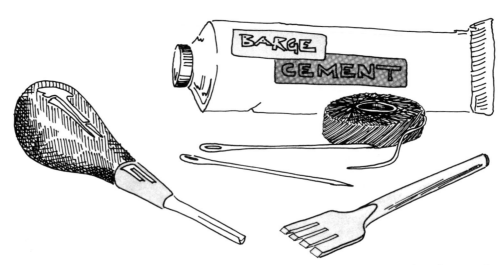

Sheathmaking requires only simple equipment. Shown here are a tube of cement, a thonging chisel, a grooving tool, large needles, and a spool of waxed linen thread.

fish or animal oils. Vegetable tanning uses organic material such as tree bark. Since the bark of oak trees was the traditional source for the tannin used in vegetable tanning, this leather is sometimes called *oak-tanned.*

Any of these methods produce clean, strong leather, but only vegetable-tanned hides have the ability to be formed (molded when wet) and embellished with surface decoration through stamping or tooling. The second sheath discussed here can be made of any of the above since it involves neither of these techniques, but the other two sheaths in this chapter are molded and require vegetable-tanned leather.

The other materials needed for sheathmaking are quite simple and can usually be bought wherever you get the leather. You'll need a heavy *needle,* a tough thread called *waxed linen,* a *thonging chisel,* some rubber-based *cement* (e.g. *Barge Cement*), and some snaps. You'll also need a sharp *utility knife.* You might want to use a small *grooving tool* but this is optional.

The first step is, of course, to figure out what kind of sheath you want. The patterns shown here are given as a point of reference to get you started, but you'll enjoy the challenge of coming up with original sheaths to complement your original knives. Throughout this book I have stressed the importance of function in design. The purpose of a tool affects its size, shape, and material. This is true of sheaths as it is of knives. As you design a sheath, keep in mind its use, its position on the belt, and so on.

The first example shows a fold-over pouch sheath in a popular style. One drawing shows a few of the many variations on this approach. This sheath fits knives without a quillon (the part of a guard that stands out from the blade). The second example, a snap sheath, is more applicable to knives that have a quillon.

To protect the knife blade and the fingers of the sheathmaker, begin by wrapping the blade with heavy tape or aluminum foil before setting to work on the sheath. This is especially important for this first knife since water will be used in the molding process. It's not good for any knife to sit in a moist atmosphere, so be especially careful to enclose the blade completely when wrapping a knife to be used in molding.

A MOLDED POUCH SHEATH

To test the design and the size, draw a pattern on heavy paper. A split grocery bag works well. Trace the knife outline onto the paper, then draw a second line

A pouch sheath of 6-ounce cowhide, shown with Project 2.

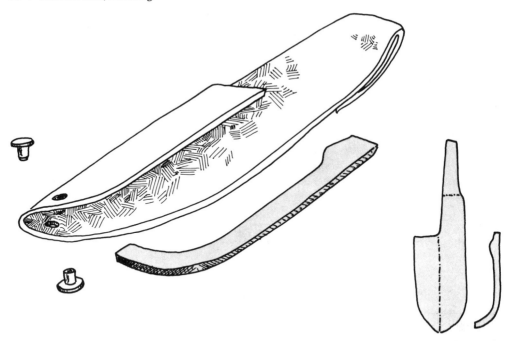

This exploded view of the pouch sheath shows its construction. The detail shows the shape of the sheath before folding.

about ⅜ inch larger than the first. This is shown in the accompanying drawing. Fold the paper down the outside line that was drawn along the spine or thick edge of the blade. Use scissors to cut the paper around the outline.

Of course the sheath as made so far would completely enclose the knife and make it difficult to withdraw. To solve this, cut away a small amount of the front of the sheath. Snip away about an inch and set the knife into the paper pattern. If there isn't enough handle sticking out to make an easy grip, trim off a little more. Continue in this way until the sheath looks and feels good.

The next thing to be built into the pattern is the belt loop. Cut a strip of paper between 1 and 2 inches wide, and fold this so it will fit easily over a belt. Most belts are between 1½ and 2½ inches wide. If the loop is broad and makes a close fit to the width of the belt, the sheath will resist flapping from side to side as it is worn.

Lay this strip of paper onto the paper pattern to find a position that will secure the sheath comfortably below the belt. At the same time, see that it is in proportion to the rest of the sheath. Tape or glue the strip into position. This completes the paper pattern. Once you have the idea, the sheath pattern can be figured out in a single step and quickly cut from paper.

The sewn side of the sheath requires a spacer called a *welt*. The thickness of this piece of leather will depend on the heft of the knife. If necessary, it's possible to use two or three thicknesses of whatever leather you have on hand to make up the desired thickness. Keep in mind that the molding of this sheath will cause it to swell outward. Usually a single thickness of 6- to 8-ounce leather is sufficient for the welt.

The shape of the welt is easily found by tracing the edge of the sheath pattern and the blade of the knife. The welt will be even with the sheath on the outside and have a clearance of about ⅛ inch from the blade. In this example I have included a bulge in the welt near the top. This will rub against the guard of the knife and increase friction against the handle. This helps to hold the knife in the sheath.

When the pattern pieces have been cut

out of paper, give them a trial fit over the knife. Keep in mind that because the paper is thinner than the leather, the fit at this stage should be quite loose. If everything seems to be in order the pattern is traced onto the leather with a felt marker, on the side of the skin that won't show in the finished sheath. In these examples I'm turning the rough or flesh side in, but of course it's possible to show that side. Cut the leather with a sharp knife, being careful to stay on the lines.

The belt loop is folded over and secured into place. This is achieved with both glue and stitches, in that order. Leather is glued with flexible contact cement. Read the instructions on the

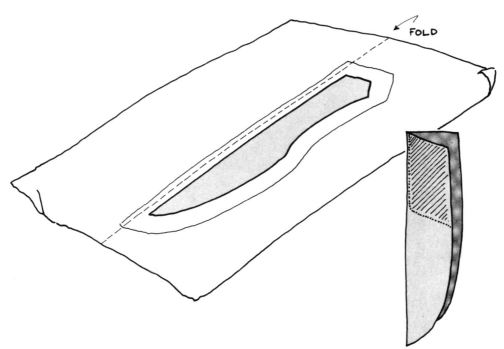

Begin the sheath by tracing the knife onto heavy paper. After folding, cut out a pattern at least ⅜-inch larger than the knife. As shown in the inset, a piece of the front flap is cut away to make an opening for the pouch.

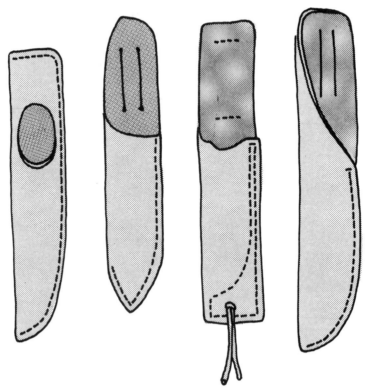

Some other designs for a folded pouch sheath.

cement and follow them carefully. The first step is to spread the cement onto both of the surfaces being joined. Allow it to dry until it is tacky, then press the parts together. Contact cement is a one-chance operation: *the parts cannot be shifted after the pieces are brought into contact.* Be certain of what you're doing before you begin.

The pieces may be clamped while drying but this is not usually necessary. Be careful to avoid spreading excess glue around the joint area since it's difficult to clean up. To ensure that contact is thorough, some leatherworkers use a mallet to pound the joint together.

When the glue has set, which will take

at least several hours, the bond is reinforced with stitches. Four or six will be enough to connect the tip of the loop to the body of the sheath.

Use a scribe or a small nail to pound holes in the leather through which a thick needle can be passed. Thread a short length of waxed linen thread through a needle and tie a large knot in one end of the thread. It's possible to use the thread doubled, but the result usually looks messy so I prefer to use only a single strand. Begin from the back so the knot will be out of sight. Make an orderly pattern of stitches, an X or two horizontal lines, for instance. You will go through several of the holes twice. Finish with the

needle coming out the back, loop the
thread through a couple stitches, and tie
it off.

The welt is now glued into place and
the sheath halves are folded over and
cemented at the same time. It's as easy
as following the manufacturer's directions. In this case you will probably need
to find some way to clamp the parts together. Use a vise, Vise-Grips, C-clamps,
or weights.

Allow the cement to set up as recommended, probably overnight. The seam
is then reinforced with stitches. As a preliminary step to sewing, it is possible to
cut a channel for the threads to lie in.
This will protect the thread from wear
and help achieve a tidy seam. If a channel is to be cut it is done at this stage.
Use a grooving tool or a similarly shaped
linoleum cutter, working on both the
front and the back.

The holes for sewing can be made with
a thonging chisel. This miniature pitch-
fork takes care of cutting and spacing all
at once. Of course a nail, scribe, or hole
punch could also be used. Start at the top
of the pouch by setting the chisel about
⅛ inch from the top edge and ⅛ inch in
from the edge. If a groove was made, set
the chisel into the groove. Working on a
scrap board, strike the chisel solidly
enough that it will penetrate through
the sheath and welt. This might take a
couple blows. Pull the chisel out and set
it so the end tine fits into the last hole
of the previous blow. Strike again and
continue this operation until you reach
the tip of the sheath.

The illustration shows three simple
ways to create a solid line of stitches.
In the first case the needle jumps ahead
an extra hole with each stitch so the
threads make an overlapping pattern. In

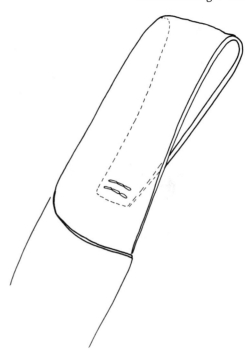

**The belt loop is folded over and fastened,
first with cement, then with a few stitches.**

the second instance the sewing makes a
simple up-and-down progression all the
way down the sheath, then turns around
and weaves its way back to the beginning, filling in the open spaces as it goes.
The third method, called a saddle stitch,
uses two needles working from opposite
sides simultaneously. Whatever method
you use, it is important to pull the thread
taut at each stitch. End the sewing by
pulling the thread tight up against several of the last stitches. Weave the loose
end through a couple stitches and tuck it
into the seam of the sheath.

In this example I reinforced the tip of
the sheath with the same kind of brass
cutler's rivet used in the handle of the
knife. I used the heavy-duty rivet sold
for knife handles, but a lighter version

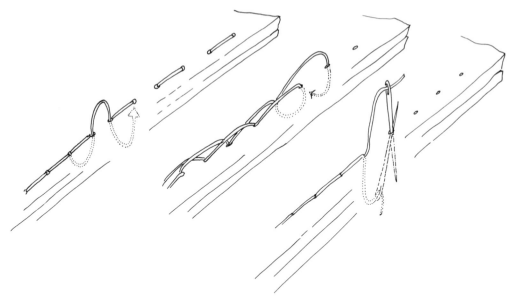

Here are several ways to make a solid line of stitches.

is available in several lengths from a leather supply company. Because of the thinness of the leather I had to cut a small piece off each rivet section before pressing the two together. For details on this operation look ahead to chapter 7.

The edge of the sheath is trimmed with a knife and then shaved or sanded smooth. A utility knife can be used to whittle away any excess and to create a smooth edge. A faster and neater job can be done by using a sanding machine and a medium-grit belt. This removes excess leather and also burnishes the edge.

To soften the leather for molding it is soaked in warm water until darkened, perhaps five minutes. Pull it from the bath and shake off excess water, then wrap the sheath in a towel and set it aside for an hour or two. This process, called "casing," allows the moisture to penetrate throughout the leather and creates a material that is uniformly flexible.

Slide the wrapped knife into the sheath and use your fingers to work the leather over the form of the blade and handle. Withdraw the knife periodically to be certain it slides in and out easily. When the sheath has taken the desired form, allow it to dry with the knife still in it. Dry it in a warm but not hot area. This could take several days and should not be rushed. Avoid direct heating because this will dry out the leather and leave it brittle.

For a final finish the sheath is rubbed with clear shoe polish, neatsfoot oil, saddle soap, or a similar commercial preparation. Penetration is enhanced if these oil and wax mixes are warm. They can be heated in a small double boiler arrangement made with tin cans and applied with a rag. Another possibility is to rub the finish into the leather vigorously with the fingers, allowing body warmth and friction to assist.

A SNAP SHEATH

The two basic joining techniques of leatherwork, gluing and sewing, are the same in this sheath as in the last. The major difference here is in the addition of a snap to secure the knife, and in the design, which stacks rather than folds pieces.

As explained before, this style of sheath is best suited to knives with quillons. The guard projecting from the handle makes the pouch style impossible but provides a feature that will hold the knife into this sheath. In this example I'm using the same 6- to 8-ounce cowhide as in the preceding sheath.

The first step is to plan out the pieces and the sequence of assembly. The illustration here should help to clarify this. When making a sheath of your own design I recommend making a similar sketch. Don't worry about a lack of draw-ing skills; this sketch is for personal reference only.

Trace the knife onto a piece of heavy paper and draw an outline at least ⅜ inch larger all the way around. Cut this out and use it to trace onto the leather. You will be laying out five pieces: a full back, a half-back, a front, a strap, and a welt. Remember that the welt can be made up of two or three thicknesses if needed. Arrange these pieces on the leather in the way that makes best use of the material. Trace the full outline for the back, the top half for the half-back, the bottom half for the front and the welt. The half-back should slide under the front by about ¼ inch. You will also need the strap that wraps around the handle. This will probably be about 4 inches long and ½ inch wide. Cut each piece out with a razor knife.

If a double welt is used, those pieces are glued and clamped. Use the knife to

A snap sheath, shown with Project 6.

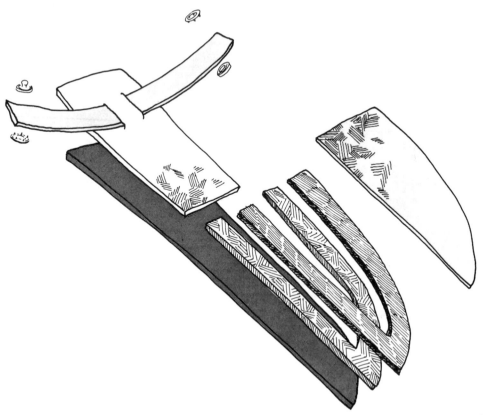

An exploded diagram showing the parts that make a layered sheath. In this example two welts are used, but one is generally enough.

A rugged knife and sheath by Tom Barminsky. The blade is 440C and the handle is of Pakkawood. (Photo courtesy of the artist)

cut a gradual bevel (called a *skive*) onto the lower edge of the half-back piece. This will make a smoother transition where it joins the back. Next make two slits in the half-back and slide the strap through it. You can make a slightly neater job by punching a small hole at the top and bottom of each slot.

Apply cement to the half-back (avoiding the strap area), to both sides of the welt, and to the outer edges of the front. As explained before, allow the glue to dry until tacky, then press and clamp. Remember that the pieces cannot be shifted once they have been touched together.

After the glue has dried, use the thonging chisel to cut a series of slots in the leather all the way around the outside of the sheath. When making sharp corners you may need to switch to a narrower chisel or modify by doubling two or three tines into previously cut holes. It may be necessary to go over the slots from the back in a second course of hammering to enlarge the holes enough to let a needle to go through.

Start the needle inside the opening of the sheath, again working so the knot on the end of the thread is buried inside the sheath. Stitch all the way around using any of the sewing techniques illustrated above. Tie off the thread when done and work the loose end back into the seam.

Slide the knife into the sheath and measure the strap around the handle.

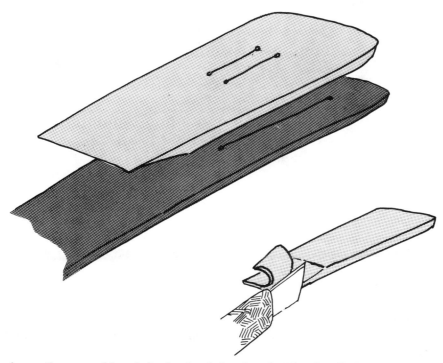

This shows the assembly of the back of the sheath. The detail shows the process of "skiving," or beveling an edge to make a smoother fit between two pieces.

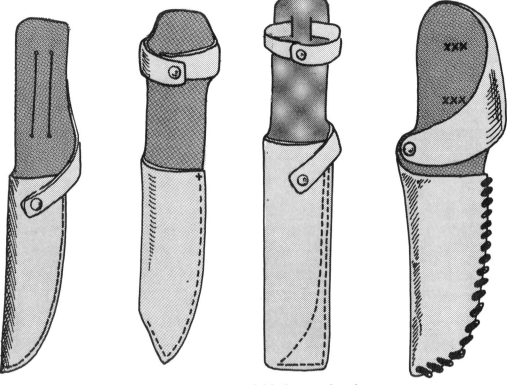

Some variations on folded snap sheaths.

The fit should be comfortably loose, easy enough to open and close with one hand. Allow about ½ inch overlap for the snap and cut the strap to length.

Snaps are bought from a leather supply house and are usually available in at least a couple sizes and weights. I recommend the heaviest grade in any case, but the size will depend on the scale of the sheath. The snap consists of four pieces: a male and a female component, each with a washer to hold it onto the leather. These work by a simple press fit, almost like a staple. When the two units are held in alignment and squeezed, six or eight prongs are forced through the leather and into the snap, where they bend over. Use a mallet or cushioned pliers to squeeze the parts together.

As before, the sheath is finished by trimming off the uneven edges on a power sander or with a sharp knife. To preserve the finish of the leather and improve its waterproof qualities, use a wax or oil finish such as mink oil, neatsfoot oil, or neutral shoe polish.

A MOLDED POCKET SHEATH

This third example, a sheath for a folding knife, illustrates the use of a molding form. The leather was shaped over wooden blocks before the pieces were assembled. This allows for a greater

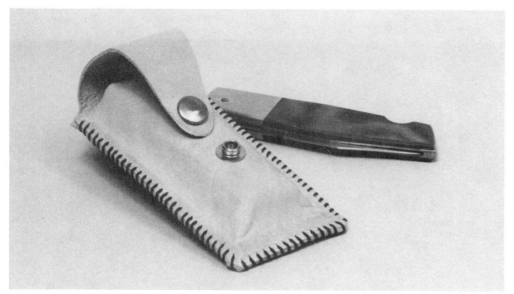

A molded sheath. Though this example is for a folding knife, Project 9, the molding process can be used on sheaths of any size.

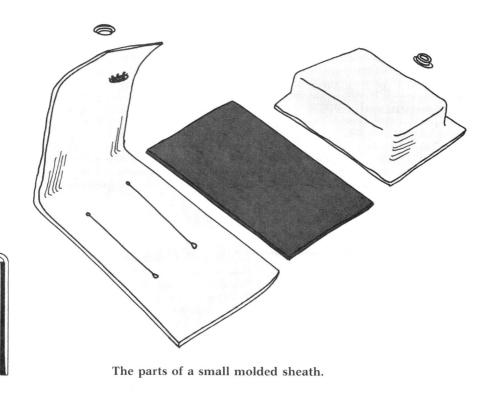

The parts of a small molded sheath.

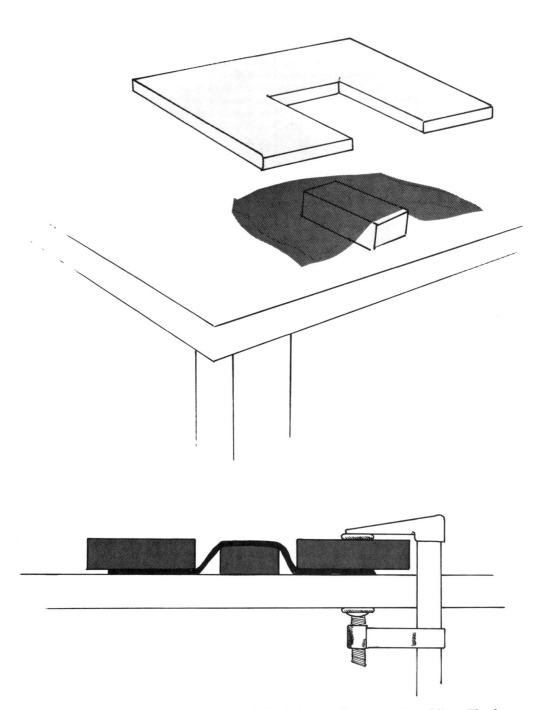

Dampened leather is laid over a small block in the first step of molding. The larger top block is set into position and clamped down as shown.

stretch in the leather than in the pouch sheath shown above. The technique of block molding is not limited to small sheaths like this one and can be used effectively in many designs.

The first step is to design a sheath and figure out how the pieces will fit together. As shown in the sketch, this example uses a single piece for the back and the front flap. Slits in the back piece make a strap for a belt.

The front of the sheath was molded between two pieces of ¾-inch plywood. Cut a rectangular opening in a piece of plywood as shown. The block that will mold the interior of the sheath is about ⅛ inch smaller than the opening on all sides. The edges of the block are smoothed and slightly beveled.

The 6- to 8-ounce cowhide used in the last two projects is too bulky for this small sheath, so I used a 4- to 5-ounce leather. As mentioned above, you must use vegetable-tanned leather because oil- and chrome-tanned material cannot be molded.

The full piece of leather, larger than will be needed, is moistened. After soaking in warm water for a couple minutes,

wrap the leather in a towel and let it sit for two hours. This allows the moisture to penetrate the leather evenly.

Lay the small block on a workbench and position the leather over it. Set the larger piece of plywood over the block and push it into position, stretching the leather. Clamp it in place with C-clamps, or secure it with weights. Let the leather dry for several days. When the clamps are removed and the block lifted off, the leather will be permanently molded into a boxy shape.

Use a razor knife to cut the pieces for the sheath. Glue these together as described above. After the glue has set, punch holes and stitch as before. In this example I used a wrap-around stitch, but any kind of stitch can be used.

After sewing, trim and smooth the edges. Set the knife into the sheath to determine the best length for the front flap. Mark and cut this, then plan the location of the snap. The pieces of each snap are laid into position. Either squeeze the parts with cushioned pliers or tap them with a mallet. As described above, the sheath is finished with neatsfoot oil or a similar sealer.

5

Forge Set-Up

It's impossible to write about knifemaking without mentioning blacksmithing. Both historically and technically, the two topics are so interrelated that it is difficult to draw a meaningful line between them. It is not within the scope of this book to teach blacksmithing, but this chapter will attempt to offer an introduction to the world of the blacksmith and will provide an opportunity for a student of knifesmithing to get a taste of the pleasures of working at a forge.

We can define blacksmithing as the art and science of shaping iron or steel while at red heat. This ancient and venerable craft can be reduced to three elementary components: the fire, the anvil, and the hammers. This chapter will describe the use and control of these elements and explain how a beginner can get started without making a big investment. For further and more detailed information, consult any of the several texts on blacksmithing listed in the bibliography.

THE FIRE

Throughout history literally hundreds of hearth configurations and fuels have been used for blacksmithing. The most common devices used today consist of a cast-iron bowl called a *firepot* set into a metal table called the *forge*. This is connected to a source of driven air, usually a hand-cranked impelled blower or a small squirrel cage blower driven by an electric motor. This latter is often fitted with a rheostat to control the amount of air being fed to the fire. In the case of a hand crank, the speed and use of the crank will determine the heat of the fire. Some smiths say they have more control over the fire with a hand crank, but most will agree that there are times when the automation of an electric motor to relieve the monotony of turning the crank is a welcome addition to the forge. An alternate way to regulate the flow of air uses a sheet of metal called a blast gate. This is either a sliding or a pivoting door, set into the pipe that brings air into the firepot. It lifts out of the way when fully open, but can be partially closed to block some of the air flow.

The list of suppliers includes a company that sells blacksmithing equipment. Anyone who is serious about blacksmithing should go to this or a similar source and buy the right equipment for the job. I have also seen small forges come up for sale at farm auctions. The drawing here illustrates a typical portable forge. Getting one of these in good condition for under $100 would be a good buy.

In order to give this book its broadest appeal I have experimented with an inexpensive do-it-yourself forge and will show here how to make and use it. It's a peculiar beast and has drawn a lot of smirks from real blacksmiths, but it works. It was used to make the forged camp knife, the vegetable chopper, and the Damascus steel blade shown in this book. The illustration shows the forge I made for under $30. You will discover many variations as you build your own and you might be able to cut the cost by using materials already on hand. The forge will need to be on solid ground, near a source of electricity and away from highly combustible surfaces. It can be indoors, but because of the large amount of stinky smoke that is produced, an outdoor setting is preferred. Hot sparks will be thrown off during forging, especially in the making of Damascus steel, so the

A commercially made portable forge. This small forge offers an inexpensive and practical heat source for a beginning knifemaker. They are available new and can sometimes be found for sale at farms or small industries.

floor must be concrete or, if wood, old enough that a speckling of black spots won't be a problem. In the case of a wooden floor, care must be taken at the end of each work day to sweep up any smoldering bits of steel to prevent the risk of a fire.

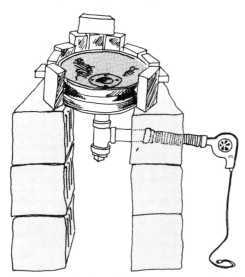

A homemade forge that uses a car wheel for the firepot. The rim is lined with fireclay and fitted with steel pipe and a hair dryer. It doesn't look like much, but it does the job.

The firepot is made within a discarded tire rim. These can be found at a junk yard or local garage and should cost only a few dollars. Be sure to mention that a damaged rim will suit your needs. In my forge I set this up between two pillars made of three cinder blocks each.

The tuyere (pronounced "twee-yar") is the blowpipe through which a blast of air enters the forge. In this case it is made of 2-inch steel plumbing pipes. The vertical pipe slides up through the rim hole intended for the car axle and is held in place by screwing a flange onto the pipe. This pipe is set into position before the pot is lined. The lower unit, the T and the pipe leading to the air supply, can be added later.

The lining of the pot is made with fireplace mortar, purchased from a brickyard. I found that a number of refractory cements are manufactured and some of these can get expensive. I made my forge with a generic mortar, ready-mixed and sold in a plastic barrel that held 20 pounds. It cost $8 and has worked well. To plug the holes in the rim and take up some of the volume, I used pieces of firebrick. Small stones or pieces of paving brick will also work. These were laid into position and the cement was pressed over them. Consult the label for advice on the drying of the cement; it might take several days. If it is laid down in one thick layer the cement is likely to crack as it dries. By checking the forge periodically as it dried I found I could push these cracks closed and the result was satisfactory. To avoid this cracking entirely, build up the cement in layers over the course of a week, dampening each layer before the next is applied. The difference is more a matter of looks than function, since the cracks soon fill with ash and do not diminish the heat of the forge.

The source of forced air in this forge is nothing fancier than a conventional hair dryer. In order to remove it from the heat of the forge, I used a 2-foot length of flexible dryer hose. The whole assembly was connected with heavy-duty tape. When I first tried my forge I found that the blower, even at its low speed, was too fast for the forge. It caused the fire to burn hot and use coal quickly. I covered up half of the air intake section of the hair dryer with a piece of tape and found that this helped reduce the force of the blow.

As can be seen in the illustration, the pipe arrangement below the firepot provides for the dumping of ashes and *clinkers*, the unburned residue of coal. To prevent these and live coals from falling through the tuyere, a piece of heavy screen or a couple short sections of steel rod are set across the opening. Since the fire is directed upward by the force of the blast these are shielded from intense heat and will survive many uses of the forge before they need to be replaced.

If your forge is exposed to the weather, always remove the plug between uses. If you forget to do this, rainwater will sit in the pipe and soon rust it tight. This makes it difficult to remove ashes.

FUEL

The best fuel for a blacksmith's forge is coal. This forge will operate well with charcoal but the fire is not hot enough for working large pieces of steel and the cost is high. Blacksmithing is best done with bituminous coal, a grade that is not as hard as the shiny lumps called anthracite. A local coal company should have an appropriate material in stock, or will be able to recommend an alternative fuel. The coal you get will be dusty and soft. It is commonly sold by weight and will probably cost about 10 cents per pound. For the small quantity you will need, bring your own containers. Plastic buckets make a handy choice. If nothing else is available, you can make a fire with the harder coal sold for use in coal fur-

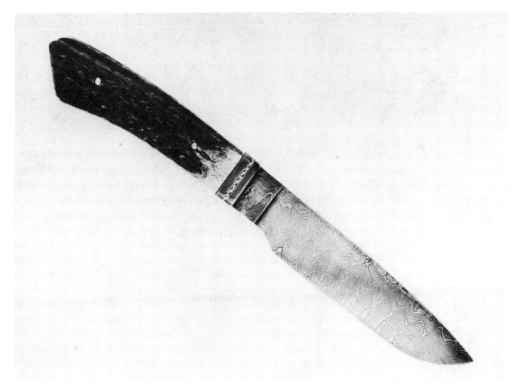

A ladder pattern Damascus hunter with an 8½-inch blade, by Barry L. Davis. The blued steel guard includes a liner of nickel silver, decorated with file work. The handles are of stag. (Photo courtesy of the artist)

naces, but be warned that it is more difficult to light than the bituminous and will require a little more tending. When you get the hang of it, though, it produces a high temperature and a clean fire.

A typical analysis of bituminous coal would show about 60 to 80% carbon, 10 to 30% volatile matter, and 7 to 10% ash. As the forge burns, the volatile matter is quickly removed. The carbon gives the heat. What's left, the ash and solid chunks of gritty stone called clinkers, are all that need to be thrown away. The first step in making a blacksmith's fire is to burn off the volatile matter to make a material called *coke*. This process, called "coking," is described below.

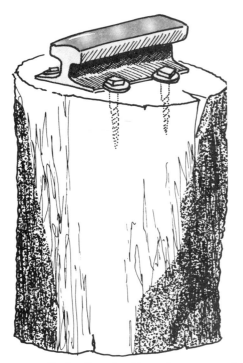

An anvil of railroad rail can be mounted on a heavy log like this.

TOOLS

The heart of a blacksmith's shop is the anvil. This ancient device has gone through few modifications since the days of the armorers of the Middle Ages. It is a classic example of pure function. To be most effective the anvil should be heavy enough to remain stable under use. Something like 150 pounds is a popular size. It should be mounted at a proper height and should be located close enough to the forge to make a comfortable swing from one work station to the next.

The height can be easily determined by holding your arm loosely at your side with the hand shaped as a fist. The top of the anvil should be even with your knuckles. A striking surface that is too high or too low will reduce the power of your blows and cause fatigue. Even when you're doing it right blacksmithing can cause fatigue, so it makes sense to set up the equipment in the most efficient way possible.

Knifesmiths who find themselves serious about forging will soon want to acquire an anvil. They can be bought new but it's a lot cheaper to find an old one, even if it has cleaned up on the surface. Farms, old factories, service stations, and scrap yards are all good places to find an anvil. Be happy if you can find one for under $1 a pound. A new anvil will probably cost about $4 a pound.

For the purpose of getting a feeling for blacksmithing, a section of railroad rail will make a workable anvil. These can be found at a scrapyard or foundry. It is especially important when using this lighter piece of steel that it be solidly mounted. If the anvil is jumping away from you at each blow you'll hold back on the hammering and that's hardly the way to flatten steel. Rig up a short sturdy table or a stump, and clamp or strap the rail into place. This is recommended for any anvil under 150 pounds. The drawing shows one possibility for setting up an improvised anvil.

An important ingredient of proper work at the anvil lies in using the right hammer. You will need a hammer that is heavy enough to work for you but not too heavy to be controlled. It must be comfortable and should have a flat face and a cross-peen. None of these qualities has anything to do with cost. You can find expensive hammers that don't work and inexpensive ones that do. The difference is largely in how you prepare the hammer before you put it to work.

The drawing here shows a typical forging hammer as it has been modified for comfortable long-term use. The dotted line indicates the handle as it came from the manufacturer. If you buy a hammer from a flea market or similar source the handle may be makeshift or altogether missing. Don't let a detail like this dissuade you from buying the hammerhead if it's the right size and shape. Replacement handles can be bought at a hardware store and are easily fitted. To secure a handle into a head, use wooden wedges and glue them in place with a white glue like Elmer's.

The handle is cut to a comfortable length and shaped with a file or rasp. When the shape is achieved, the wood should be sanded to remove any potential splinters. I usually leave the wood untreated after shaping, allowing a finish of dirt and finger oils to seal the wood. Linseed oil could be used to keep the handle better looking. During use, keep in mind that the handle shape may need to be further modified. If you are getting blisters or cramped muscles along your forearm, the solution may be a simple matter of thinning the handle or removing a bulge. Time given over to customizing a handle is always well spent.

To set the workpiece into the fire and hold it while it is being forged, you'll need a pair of tongs. A fully equipped blacksmith's shop might have upwards of a hundred pairs of tongs, each one made to

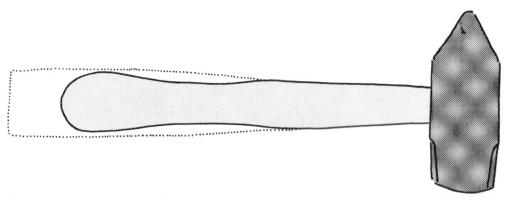

Commercial hammer handles are often too long and too thick for comfortable use at the forge. The dotted line shows one way to modify a forging hammer. Even a small adjustment can mean the difference between getting or avoiding a cramped forearm.

Large dagger by Tom Maringer. The guard, bolster, and pommel are of nickel silver, and the handle is made of wrapped fiber. (Photo courtesy of the artist)

hold a special shape. To get started, a simple pair with a flat grip will suffice. Tongs can be bought from a blacksmithing supply company (see the suppliers list) and are sometimes available at flea markets and auctions. A popular size is 18 inches long. For a knifesmith's relatively small work they should be lightweight. To get started, a cheap pair of second-hand tongs are all you need, but if you decide to continue in blacksmith-

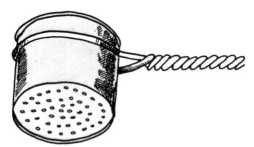

To sprinkle water onto the fire, punch holes in a tin can with a nail. The handle should be at least 2 feet long to avoid being burned by the cloud of steam that is created when dampening. Keep this in a bucket or barrel of water near the forge.

ing you'll soon want to buy or make a first-rate pair of tongs.

A small fireplace shovel or garden trowel will come in handy, and you'll need a metal scrub bucket. You should also have a perforated tin can on a handle as shown here and a stiff steel brush. These are the only tools that are needed for the projects described in this book. A class or book in blacksmithing will allow you to expand your smithy, and with it, your skills.

USING THE FORGE

Just like a good cook in the kitchen, the first step is to lay out all the materials before starting. In a convenient workspace and within reach of the anvil, be sure you have:

the forge, plugged in and working
a bucket of coal, probably about 10 to
    15 pounds per work session
a cross-peen hammer
a coarse wire brush for removing scale
Vise-Grips

a vise (optional but handy)
a bucket of water
newspaper and matches
work gloves

And while you're at it, look around to be sure that there is nothing combustible close at hand. Proper clothing would include heavy shoes, socks, long pants, and a long-sleeved shirt. Fabrics made with synthetic fibers like rayon are not recommended since they melt when hit with a spark. When the stage is set, it's time to turn up the lights.

The fire is started with a couple pieces of balled-up newspaper. Set this in the center of the firepot and cover it with a mound of coal. Some smiths also add a few pieces of kindling wood beneath the coal. This is an especially good idea if the coal is damp, or when using anthracite coal. Light the paper at several points around its edges, and allow it to grow to a full flame. Turn on the blower as slowly as possible. After about a minute, add more coal to the top of the mound with a small shovel. Within the next minute or so the fire should start producing a great deal of smelly yellowish smoke. Add more coal to the top of the mound. The correct fire will look like a hill of coal, with thick smoke oozing out all over it and small tongues of yellow flame breaking through here and there. Allow the fire to burn like this for several minutes. If there is a common error among beginning blacksmiths, it is playing with the fire too much. Like the watched pot, the fire will do best if it is left alone.

The smoke is the result of the burning off of the 10 to 30% of the coal that is volatile matter. It's messy and doesn't give much heat, so the sooner it can be gotten rid of the better. The material

that's left after this burning-out process is called *coke*. Throw a couple more shovelfuls of coal onto the fire, and while you're at it lay in a supply of coal around the periphery of the fire. This coal should be thoroughly dampened with water. To do this, fill the perforated can from the bucket and dribble water over the coal. The heat of the forge will burn off the volatile components in the coal and the water will keep this operation from being a smoky mess. As the fuel in the firepot is expended it is replaced with this coke from around the edge of the fire. More coal is then set up to be coked and the cycle continues.

With a piece of steel rod, gently prod a peephole into the fire. At its center you should see a red-orange core of brightly burning embers. These will be so intense that you'll see spots if you stare at them for too long (which is not a good idea). This core is where the fire is its hottest and where the steel will be laid to bring it to forging heat.

The duration of the fire will depend on the quality of the coal, the force of the blast, the size of the tuyere, the insulating qualities of the forge, and the practice of the smith. In other words it's hard to say just how long this fire is going to last. When the steel is being heated, that is, actively being brought to a red heat in preparation for striking with a hammer, the blower should be on. At that stage the coal is being rapidly consumed. Just before the steel is withdrawn from the fire, the blower is turned off. At this stage a modest mound of coal, if left without any further forced air, would keep burning for several hours.

One of the most easily perceived differences between a beginning and a master blacksmith is the amount of forming

A push dagger by Stephen C. Schwarzer. The Damascus steel is set off by the twisted shank and carved ivory handle. The sheath is made of nickel silver and African frog skin. (Photo by Weyer of Toledo)

that the master accomplishes in a single *heat*, or trip from the fire. This is the result of confident hammer control and also has a lot to do with being tuned in to the rhythm of the process. Part of the excitement of forging comes from the imposed pace. The steel is cooling all the time it is away from the fire. This forces the smith to devise a work method that wastes no gesture.

Another difference between the master and the beginner is that the beginner often pulls the steel out too soon. This means that the steel is not as soft as it can get. More hammer blows are needed to achieve the same amount of flattening. Pulling the steel out too soon also shortens the working time.

When you are done working with the forge, the common practice is to simply let the fire go out. If you will be firing up again within a couple days, pile coal high on the fire. This will turn into coke and give you a head start on your next fire. If you don't want to make coke, just pull any usable coal off the fire and let the rest burn itself out. Either way, the blower is turned off. It's always a good habit to check around the forge to be sure there are no fire hazards before closing up for the day. Plan a few extra minutes in your schedule to take a slow walk around the studio to make sure there are no smoldering embers in the shop.

THE GOAL OF GOOD FORGING

The goal of forging is to create the intended shape in the most efficient way with the least amount of damage to the material. Forging is a blend of engineering and artistry. The smith must know about the phases of steel, the effects of heat and quenching and the various attributes of a range of alloys. But more than that, the smith needs an intuitive sense of what shapes the steel can be made to assume. Like a potter or a glassblower, the blacksmith is always one step ahead of the material, guiding it toward a vision.

We all know that there is no teacher like experience. This is as true at the forge as anywhere else, maybe more true here than elsewhere. Experience is not just a matter of doing things, but of learning from doing things. After a little experimentation with the forge you will begin to get a sense – if you're paying attention – to the possibilities of each piece of steel. You will learn how wide a blade can be made from a ½-inch rod, how long a handle is needed to keep you comfortably away from the fire, and so on. Part of good forging is being tuned in to these lessons.

Another part of good forging is the efficient use of gestures as described above. Despite the popular image of the blacksmith as a hulking muscle-bound giant, there is a lot of the dance to good smithing. By being aware of this graceful aspect of forging you will more easily recognize it as you experience it. And this pleasure is part of good smithing too.

6

Project 1:

Kitchen Paring Knife

I don't think there is anyone over the age of ten who hasn't used a paring knife. This simple and elegant tool is, in a way, the essence of what knives are all about. It is totally practical. A good paring knife is a pleasure to use, while a cheap or dull one is a glaring frustration. In this project, you'll learn the basic skills of knifemaking: sawing, filing, riveting, and heat-treating. And you'll end up with a very handy, very special knife.

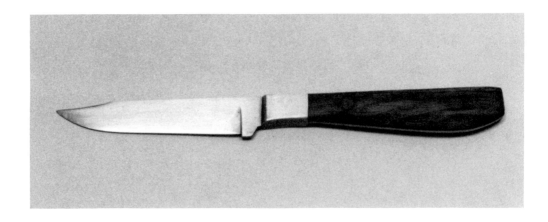

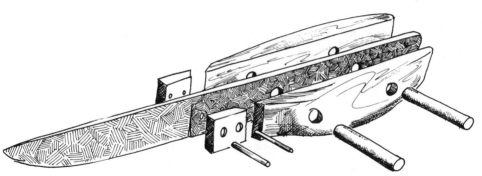

Exploded diagram of kitchen paring knife.

LIST OF MATERIALS

Blade: any hardenable tool steel (01, 440C, W2, etc.) 1/16" x 3/4" x 8"

Bolsters: about two square inches of 1/8" brass sheet; nickel silver could also be used

Handle Slabs: two pieces of wood, about 3/8" x 1" x 5"; Micarta or Pakkawood could also be used

Rivets: a couple inches of 16 gauge (3/64") brass wire

Pins: a couple inches of 1/4" wood dowel

Principal Tools: sawframe and blades, drill, drill bits and abrasive papers, heat-treating equipment

PROCESS OVERVIEW

1. Design the knife and make a full-size drawing.
2. Glue the drawing onto the steel and cut out the blade silhouette.
3. File the edges to refine the outline shape.
4. Locate and file a line to mark the ricasso from the blade (optional).
5. File the taper of the blade, removing metal from both sides evenly.
6. Saw out the bolsters.
7. Drill holes in the steel; two 1/16-inch holes for the bolster and two 1/4-inch holes for the handle slabs.

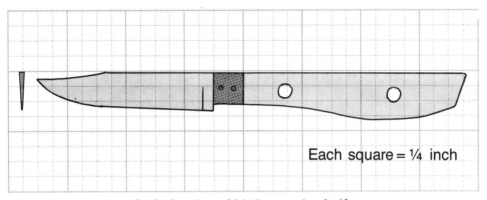

Each square = 1/4 inch

Scale drawing of kitchen paring knife.

8. Harden and temper the blade.
9. Sand the blade to the desired finish (say #400).
10. Set the bolsters into position and file them even with the blade on the top and bottom edge.
11. Remove the bolster pieces from the knife, realign with pins, and file the pieces so they are even on the front and back edges.
12. Rivet the bolsters onto the knife.
13. Trace the handle outline onto each slab; cut out the handle pieces.
14. Drill each slab to line up with the ¼-inch holes in the tang.
15. Coat the handle area with epoxy and set slabs into place, using dowels. Clamp in position.
16. After the glue has set, use rasps, files and sandpaper to shape the handle to a comfortable contour. Sand until the surface is smooth and free of marks.
17. Coat the handle with linseed or mineral oil.
18. Sharpen the blade.

DESIGN CONSIDERATIONS

Because a knife is a functional tool, it makes sense to begin by examining the function for which it is intended. A paring knife is designed to cut, peel, and slice food. It should be large enough to get the job done, but compact enough to be easily controlled. Because it will be frequently washed, it should be made of materials that will not be damaged by water.

A sharp stone satisfies all these requirements. The hope is to improve on that primitive tool. The knife being made here has a bolster to add strength and balance and a handle to make it comfortable to hold. It should be pleasing to look at, but it is a study in pure function.

To begin the design process, examine the paring knives you already own. Check to see which ones are comfortable and easy to control. Observe how well or how poorly they fit your hand. Does the full length of the blade get used, or is it too long? Do your fingers get tired soon, or is the grip relaxed and easy to maintain? When you pick up the knife, does it fall into your hand in a natural way, instantly ready for use?

PROCESS DETAIL

[1] With all this in mind, trace one of your kitchen knives onto paper. Alter the

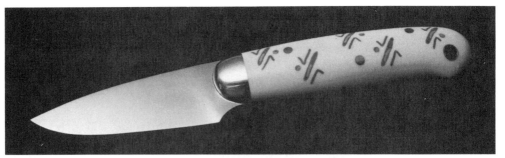

A utility knife by Peter Jagoda. The blade is made of 01 steel; the handle is Micarta with brass and epoxy. The total length is 6 inches. (Photo courtesy of the artist)

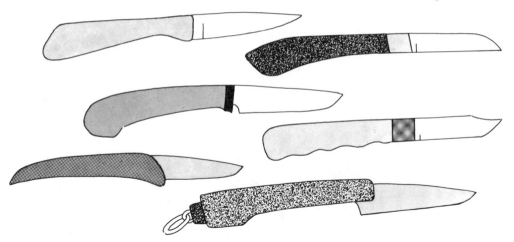

Some further ideas for paring knife designs.

traced outline to reflect your personal improvements. When you have decided on a shape, you may want to cut it out of heavy cardboard to get the feel of it in your hand. Take whatever time is necessary to be certain you have designed a comfortable blade. This might take a few tries. Remember that time spent here will be repaid many times over in the value of a well-designed knife.

[2] When the design is established it is ready to be transferred onto the metal. This can be done by gluing your drawing directly onto the metal. Use rubber cement or a household glue such as Elmer's. I've had good luck with a sticky-back white paper used by print shops to make labels. This is a tough paper with a uniform coating of adhesive. Whichever method you use, it is important to clean the steel of its oily skin before you try to get anything to stick to it. Do this by rubbing it with fine sandpaper or a kitchen scouring pad.

Sawing

As explained in chapter 1, there are several popular ways to cut out a blade shape. The method I prefer uses a jeweler's sawframe, a workbench, and a little practice. This is the method I have used to make all the projects shown in this book.

One advantage of this method is that it is inexpensive. Low cost by itself is not automatically a virtue, but it makes knifemaking that much easier to pick up as a hobby. Also, the sawframe is incredibly versatile. It can be used to cut broad strokes in thick material or delicate tracery in thin stock. It is used on metal, wood, plastic, and just about everything else. With practice it can cut to tolerances as fine as the eye can perceive. And finally, it is an accomplished art. It feels good when you get the hang of it. When mastered, sawing becomes as lyrical and fulfilling as an athletic pursuit. Like

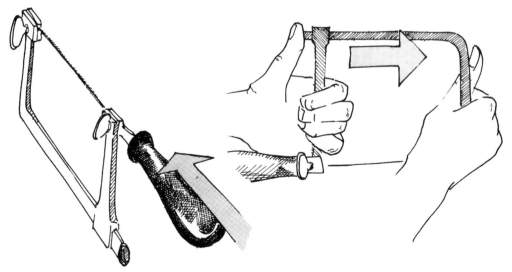

Two ways of inserting a saw blade. In the example on the left, push the sawframe against the edge of a workbench to compress the frame. Hold it there while the blade is set into position. The other example shows how to stretch a frame when the blade is in place. The thumb of the left hand holds the frame taut while the thumbscrew on the top is tightened.

athletics, it's not going to come without a little practice.

Understanding the frame and its use is quite simple. Practice is needed more than instruction. The first step is to get the blade properly loaded into the frame. I can suggest two methods to do this.

Look closely at the blade and hold it so that the teeth point *toward* the handle. Grip the blade in the plate away from the handle, as shown. Set the length of the frame so the tip of the blade just reaches the other gripping plate. The screw on the back of the frame is tightened to fix this length. With the front tip of the frame resting on the edge of the workbench, lean into the frame so that it bends a little. While leaning, slide the loose end of the blade into place beneath the gripping plate and tighten the thumbscrew.

When you release pressure the frame will spring out, putting the blade under tension. Test the tautness of the blade by plucking it like a guitar string. If you don't hear a sharp ping, try the procedure again.

Another method to achieve the same end starts by securing the blade beneath gripping plates at each end. Again the teeth must point toward the handle. Loosen the thumbscrew on the back of the frame and pull the frame open as shown. Set your thumb on the end of the frame back to hold it in position while you tighten the thumbscrew. Check by plucking as before.

Sawing is done on a piece of wood that projects about 4 inches straight out from the front of the workbench. This is called a bench pin; it can be bought from a

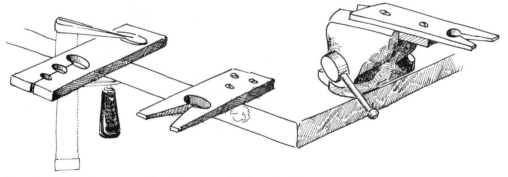

Bench pins and mounts for them can be bought from any supplier of jewelry equipment. Here are a few substitutes you can rig up yourself.

jewelers' supply company or improvised as shown. For most people the best height for this is mid-chest. Sit so the shoulder of the hand you will be sawing with is in line with the bench pin. Make yourself comfortable and hold the sawframe loosely. Try to avoid the tendency to squeeze the saw handle, because the result will be broken blades, irregular cutting, and a frustrating experience. Keep the blade vertical. Don't get into the habit of a rocking or "seesawing" stroke. Hold the metal firmly, supported close to the area being cut. You might find that the holding is the hardest work of cutting. Often the first muscles to tire are the fingers that hold the piece being cut. With an hour or two of practice you'll find sawing to be a fluid, relaxing activity.

The saw is capable of making precise turns, but this requires a special technique. If you turn the blade too much in one up-and-down stroke it will break. Instead, the blade "marches in place" as the turn is made. The frame continues to move up and down as the blade is slowly

This photo illustrates the correct position for sawing. Note the paper pattern glued to the steel.

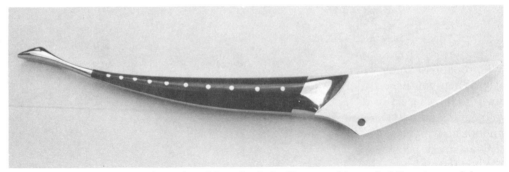

"Scrap Knife" by Michael Croft. This 9-inch knife uses 01 steel, Micarta, and brass. (Photo courtesy of the artist)

repositioned from one direction to another.

Beeswax or paraffin can be used to lubricate the sawblade. I find it handy to stick the wax onto the side of the bench pin at the point where it meets the workbench. This is done by warming the wax until its surface is gooey. For those who prefer to lubricate with a liquid, any light oil (3-in-1, Marvel Mystery, etc.) can be used. For adding a pleasant aroma to the shop I recommend Oil of Wintergreen, which is available at drugstores. Keep this in a small container filled with a sponge or a wad of fabric. Because this evaporates quickly it must be covered. Either lubricant is applied periodically while sawing.

Filing

[3] Once the knife blade has been cut out, it is time to turn this blank into a knife. The first step is to smooth away the saw marks on the edge you just cut. At the same time, the profile of the knife can be refined. Use a large file while holding the steel in a vise. In order to get

the most advantage out of the file, follow these guidelines.

Press down hard. A file cuts according to the pressure behind it. To make the most of each stroke, stand over the vise with your feet planted wide apart. In this way the torso weight gets thrown behind each stroke.

The teeth of the file point away from the handle, causing the cut to take place on the push stroke. Dragging the file back on the return stroke bends the tips of the teeth over, dulling the file and shortening its life. The proper stroke is a push-lift-return-push cycle.

Pressure can be increased by using both hands. A right-handed person will usually hold the file handle in the right hand and set the palm of the left hand on the tip of the file. Because this area is toothed, the left palm can get sore. To prevent this, wear gloves, wrap a rag around the tip of the file, or put a Band-Aid over this part of your hand before starting to file.

As you work you'll notice that the file leaves deep marks when the stroke is in one direction, but almost none when the direction is changed. This has to do with the angle of the teeth of the file. The direction showing the deepest marks is cutting the most at each stroke, so you will probably do most of your work that way. When you have trimmed the steel down to the shape you intend to use for your knife you will want an edge that is smooth and regular. Alter the direction of your stroke accordingly.

When the outline or silhouette has been smoothed all around, it is time to create the bevel of the blade by filing away material on the sides of the blank.

Holding the knife blank so it can be filed on the face of the blade requires some ingenuity. One method, shown in the drawing, uses Vise-Grips. These are clenched onto the knife blank and then in turn set into the vise. The grip must be very tight, and even at that the blank might rotate a little with your first file strokes. Line the jaws of the Vise-Grips with a piece of scrap leather to protect against scratches in the steel. When opening the Vise-Grips, be careful that they don't snap open so fast they hurt your fingers.

Another way to set up a blank for filing is to clamp it to the edge of the workbench with a C-clamp. To prevent damage to the bench top, use a scrap board as shown.

The cutting edge of the blade should be centered along the thickness of the knife. In hand filing, this is a matter of observation. Periodically turn the knife over and work evenly on both sides.

[4] Between the blade and the bolster there is often a small unsharpened area called the *ricasso*. This can be blended into the bevel of the knife but tradition-

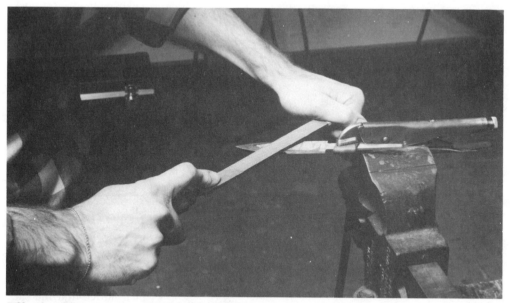

Effective filing requires a solid grip by both hands. Stand close enough to the work so you can lean into it, throwing your body weight into the stroke.

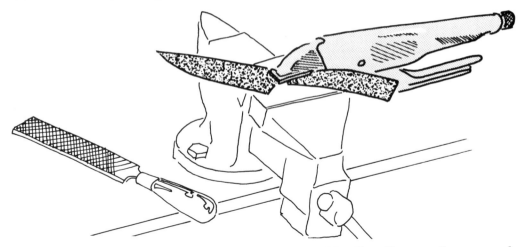

To hold a blade for filing, grip it in Vise-Grips like this. The pliers are then secured in a vise.

ally it is marked with a sharp line. The character of the line will greatly add to or detract from your knife, so take care to be neat. If you have decided on a sharp line at the edge of the ricasso, draw it onto the blank with pencil or felt tip pen. Sight along the top and bottom edge of the blade to copy the line from one side of the blade to the other. With the blank held as described above, use the edge of a file to cut a groove parallel to the line you drew, but just slightly toward the tip. Go over this again several times so that each stroke makes the line sharper and deeper. You'll find that it "grows" toward the line you drew. When you have filed

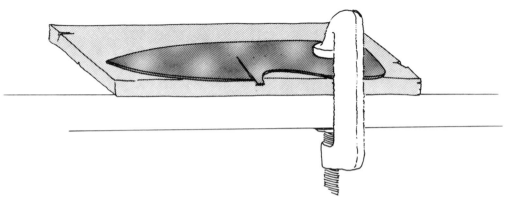

Another way to hold a blank for filing is to clamp it onto the workbench like this. To protect the bench, the blade is set on a piece of scrap wood.

halfway through the thickness of the steel, turn the blank over and repeat the process. When the ricasso line is clearly established, file from this outward (i.e. toward the tip) about a half inch, establishing the beginnings of the bevel that makes the blade. Work can now proceed on the rest of the blade, moving faster and being careful only to avoid accidently filing the ricasso section.

[5] Continue filing until the two sides meet, making the knife edge. Don't bother to try to sharpen the knife at this stage. The edge will only roll over, casting up a little burr. Before moving on to sandpaper to remove the file marks, let's examine the shape of the blade to be sure everything is in order.

Blade Shape

As explained in chapter 3, the proper shape of a blade is determined by its intended use. Because a paring knife needs to be very sharp and will not be subjected to brutal abuse, I will create a shape that favors sharpness over sturdiness. This means the blade will be thin and will taper all the way up its side.

This is shown in the scale drawing at the beginning of the chapter. It's common for beginners to misjudge the cross-section of the blade and quit filing too soon. The result will be a blade that is not especially sharp and will dull quickly. By checking periodically and working on both sides of the blade alternately, you will develop a blade that is symmetrical and properly thin.

Even though the blade has not been hardened, you can use it to do a few typical paring knife jobs in the kitchen. Try cutting up a carrot or peeling a potato. If the blade is too thick, it will feel dull and clumsy. This probably indicates that more filing is needed. If it feels good now, it will feel great when it's finished.

[6] The next step is to cut out the bolster pieces. Lay the blade onto a piece of brass sheet and trace its outline. Make marks with a felt tip pen to indicate where the bolster will go, then carry these marks over onto the reverse side of the blade. Flip the steel over and trace the second bolster shape. Saw out these two pieces.

[7] Holes are drilled in the steel to hold the bolster and the handle slabs. For the

"Knife for Exploring My Aunt's Attic" by Ken Coleman. This small knife uses 440C steel, bronze, Bocote, and copper. (Photo courtesy of the artist)

bolster, use two 1/16-inch holes. Be sure they are within the area marked for the bolster. The handle holes will be 1/4 inch, but the best way to drill them is to start with a pilot hole of a smaller diameter. The 1/16-inch bit is a handy size to use.

Drill bits have a tendency to spin off to the side as they first touch a piece. Accurate placement of the holes is achieved by making a small dimple called a *center-punch mark*. The proper tool for this (called, remarkably enough, a center-punch) can be bought at any hardware store. Any pointed tool can be used, even a nail, though it will soon bend and need to be replaced. The goal is to make a tiny crater that will locate the bit.

If you use an electric hand drill or a drill press *be sure to wear goggles*. I usually start the hole just enough to make a clear mark, then set a drop of oil into the hole. This will lubricate and cool the bit, greatly extending its life.

When all four holes have been drilled with the smaller bit, redrill the handle holes with the 1/4-inch bit, again using oil.

Hardening and Tempering

[8] Chapter 2 discusses the science of hardening steel. This section describes the process as it is done in the workshop. Another method, one that uses an open forge, is discussed in chapter 10. The process is really a simple one that involves two steps. The knife is first heated to a bright red and quenched in oil. This causes the formation of a certain crystal shape. After cleaning off the dark scale formed in that operation, the blade is heated a second time to relieve stresses. This second step is called *tempering*.

Industrially, great care is taken to maintain certain kinds of quenching oils at certain temperatures for specific steels. In our case any old motor oil will do, even recycled crankcase oil. Remember to observe commonsense rules about storing and disposing of oil safely. If you have questions, contact a local garage or the fire department.

The blade can be held in tweezers or pliers but I prefer the positive grasp of the Vise-Grips. Grip the knife at the end of the tang and lay the blade on a heat-proof

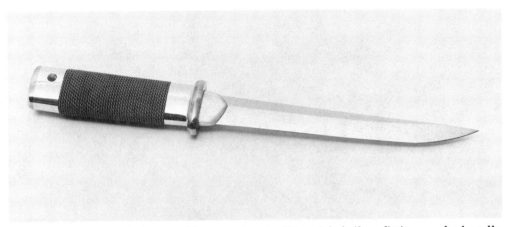

This sleek 7-inch blade by Tom Maringer is set off by nickel silver fittings and a handle of wrapped fiber. (Photo courtesy of the artist)

surface such as a firebrick. Heat it with a torch until the blade shows a bright red orange color, which will be about 1,500°F. Because it is the thinnest section, the tip of the blade can be easily overheated. Keep an eye on the tip; don't let it get white hot or give off sparks.

When the color is uniformly bright and red orange, quickly pick up the Vise-Grips and plunge the blade into a can of oil, which should be sitting nearby. As you do this, stir the oil just as if the blade were a spoon and you were cooking a pot of food. Without this motion, the blade would immediately become surrounded by an envelope of warm oil that would not cool the steel at a uniform rate. Keep the blade in the oil for a minute or two, then pull it out and wipe off the oil on a rag or paper towel.

Before going any further, check to see if this step has been successful. Stroke a file lightly against the blade. The file should slide over the blade, giving a "glassy" feel. A light pass of the file will create a high-pitched noise that is the fastest test of hardness. For a comparison sound, slide the file over the tang area. If you can't readily tell the difference between the two, repeat the hardening process.

After putting this hardness into the blade, the next step is to take some of it away. Every treatment of steel involves trade-offs, and the most common is between hardness and flexibility. At this stage the blade is as hard as it can possibly get, but it is also very brittle. So brittle, in fact, that it could break if dropped.

The blade is reheated to create a material that will hold an edge and still be flexible enough to stand up to typical kitchen use. The sophisticated heat sen-

sors of an industrial heat-treating plant are replaced in the studio by a keen eye. As the steel is heated, it forms an oxide film on its surface. The thickness of this film reflects a range of colors that go through a consistent spectrum according to temperature. It is therefore possible to "read" temperature by observing the color of the steel. Because the black scale left by the hardening process makes it difficult to see the colors, the first step is to clean away the scale. Any grit of sandpaper can be used for this.

Tempering happens quickly, so you should use a small flame. A slow process you can control is better than a fast one that you can't. Ideal tempering will create a thin strip of brass color along the edge of the blade, a plum-colored strip behind that, and a blue color over the rest of the blade. Stopping when the whole blade attains the brassy color that comes first would leave the blade brittle. Heating beyond the blue color would mean losing the edge-holding power of the steel. If the steel is overheated, go back to the beginning and repeat the hardening process.

In tempering I usually hold the blade, still in its Vise-Grip handle, in the air. Play the torch over the blade as you watch for the first sign of a golden yellow color. When this appears, "paint" the heat so the color goes all over the blade, especially toward the spine. Coax the blade through brown to plum and blue by directing the torch flame where it is needed, then quickly quench the whole blade. This quench can be in either water or oil. Whichever you use, be sure it is close at hand so not a moment is lost between torch and quench.

If you're really daring, the test of this last process is to set the blade up in a vise

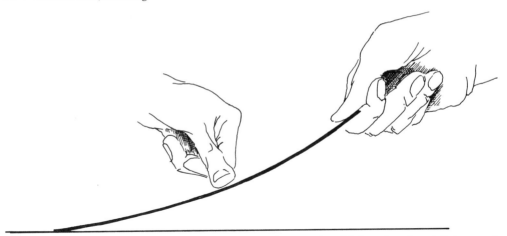

To test the tempering of a blade, flex it like this. It should bend at least this much and spring back to straight.

and pull it to see if it will bend a good distance, then spring back to straight. If it snaps off, you didn't temper enough. If it bends and doesn't spring back, you went too far. The illustration shows a more reasonable test of the knife's flexibility. If the tempering is correct, the knife will take this kind of flexing and spring back to straight. Even the small amount of bend shown here is more than the knife is likely to see in use, so if it passes this test you can feel pretty certain that your knife will last for many years.

[9] Sand the blade to the desired finish, remembering that this is largely a matter of taste. I would start with a #220 abrasive paper. This is followed by something in the 300s, and you can stop here with a frosted surface. If you want a brighter look, continue to a #400, or a #500 grit, which will give a brushed satin surface.

Bolsters

[10] Lay one of the bolster pieces into position on the blade and mark the loca-

tion of the holes to be drilled in it. Flip the blade over and do the same for the other bolster piece. Centerpunch the marks and drill the holes. Remember that these holes must make a very tight fit with the brass wire that is to be used for the pins. Either use the correct drill bit or file the wire to make the fit snug. It is not necessary to use oil when drilling brass. If the pieces are too small to hold easily in your fingers, use the Vise-Grips to hold them, using leather pads in the pliers to prevent scarring the brass.

Set the bolster pieces onto the steel. Use the two short lengths of wire to locate the bolsters. Set the knife in a vise and file the top and bottom edges of the brass until they are flush with the steel.

[11] Remove the brass from the blade, realign the two pieces with the pins, and file the front and back edges so they are even, as shown. You might want to curve the front edges down to meet the blade. The back edges might angle in to help grip the wood of the handle. Both of these modifications will add a detail of

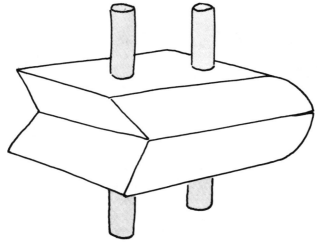

Set the bolster pieces together and align them with pins before filing the front and back edges. In this case, the rounded edge will lie on the blade and the angled area will be against the handle slabs.

craftsmanship to the knife, but neither is necessary.

[12] The bolster will be held onto the steel by two rivets. A rivet is simply a pin with a head or bulged-out mass at each end. In this case we will use short lengths of wire. If brass wire is used the rivets will blend into the bolster so well that they will almost disappear. If a contrasting metal such as copper or nickel silver is used, the rivet results in an inlaid dot.

Start by making a slight crater for the head of the rivet to fill. Use the ¼-inch drill bit to scoop out a tiny counterbore around the two holes in each bolster piece. This can be done by hand. Assemble the pieces in their correct position and slide two lengths of wire through the holes. The wire is then snipped so that

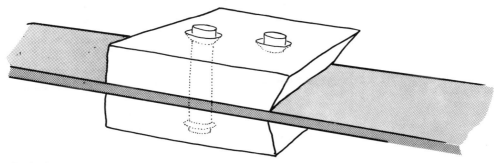

The bolster pieces ready to be riveted. The amount projecting above the surface should be equal to half the diameter of the rod. Having too much exposed can create as many problems as having too little.

about half its diameter (1/32 inch in this case) extends above the surface of the brass on either end of the wire. Set the assembly onto a steel surface, such as the top of a vise. Use the cross-peen (wedge-shaped) end of a riveting hammer to spread the metal into a head, as shown in the illustration. Lightly tap the end of the wire until it begins to spread into an oval. Turn the hammer 90 degrees and tap again. This will spread the rivet evenly in all directions. Smooth it down with a few taps of the flat-faced end of the hammer and flip the knife over so you can do the same thing to the other end of the pin. Continue flipping back and forth until the rivet heads completely fill the countersunk area. Excess metal can be filed away until the rivets are flush with the surface of the brass.

Handle Slabs

[13] Of the several materials possible for the handle, I'm going to use a hardwood. It has the advantage of a rich look, interesting grain pattern, a warm feel, and ease of shaping. The list of suppliers gives several sources for exotic woods.

Local craft stores and cabinetry shops may also be a source of supply. While any wood can be used, hardwoods will stand up to wear better than softwoods like pine, poplar, etc. Fruit woods such as apple and pear are especially well suited to use as a handle.

Cut the wood into slabs about 3/8 inch thick, and make sure one side of each piece is perfectly flat. Power saws and sanding machines make this job a quick one, but there is no reason why it can't be done by hand. File the end of the slab so it makes a tight fit with the bolster. If the bolster was angled in step 11, match the end of the handle slab to that angle.

Lay the knife onto the wood slab and trace the handle shape. Cut the wood along this line with a bandsaw, a coping saw, or a jeweler's saw.

[14] As shown here, grip one handle piece in position with Vise-Grips. Drill holes in the wood directly through the holes in the steel. Precision here is crucial. Remove the first slab and flip the knife over. Set the other slab in place and repeat the process.

[15] Rub the handle area of the steel with fine abrasive paper to remove any oils, then coat the tang with a thin film

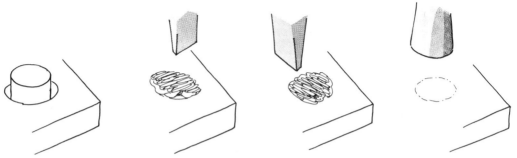

Steps in forming a rivet head. The cross-peen hammer is used to direct the flow of the metal, forcing it outwards. Rivets are an important part of knifemaking and deserve whatever practice is necessary to fully master them.

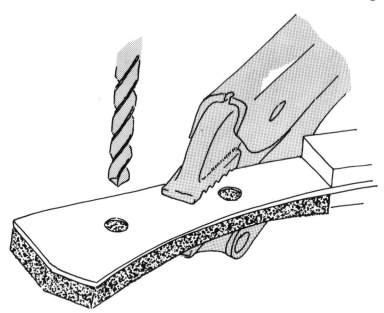

Use Vise-Grips to hold the handle slab in place while drilling.

of epoxy. Apply glue to both sides and set the wood into place. Spread a little epoxy on the dowels and slide them into position to hold the handle slabs in alignment. Set the handle into a vise or Vise-Grips and clamp while the glue dries (refer to the manufacturer's instructions).

[16] When the glue has set, cut off any excess dowel and shape the handle with rasps, files, and sandpaper. Remember to stop periodically while shaping the handle to test the feel of the knife in your hand. When the shape is comfortable, sand the handle with a fine grit abrasive paper. The results will be best if you use a flint or oxide paper made for wood rather than the silicon carbide papers used on the steel and brass. When the handle is glassy smooth (probably around #360 paper), moisten the wood with linseed oil to raise the grain and sand the handle once more.

[17] Apply a heavy coat of boiled linseed oil and allow it to penetrate into the wood. Rub off any excess and repeat the process until the oil no longer soaks in.

[18] Sharpen the blade by rubbing it on an oilstone as explained in chapter 3.

Congratulations! You've made a knife! With any luck you've had a good time, you have a knife that will give you years of service in the kitchen, and you have the urge to try something a little harder. If that's the case, move right along to the next chapter.

7

PROJECT 2:

Full-Tang All-Purpose Knife

This universal style is probably the most popular knife in the world. The size, shape, and feel all coordinate in a tool of great versatility. The fact that this is a relatively simple knife to make should not obscure its elegance. The dozens of decisions about design, materials, and craftsmanship will challenge any knifemaker and offer rewards to students of all levels. This project teaches the use of soft solder and cutlers' rivets.

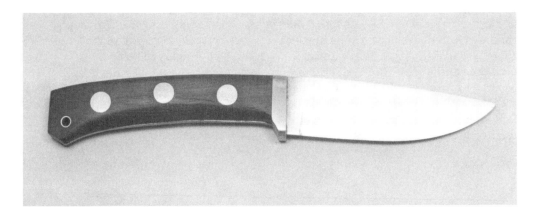

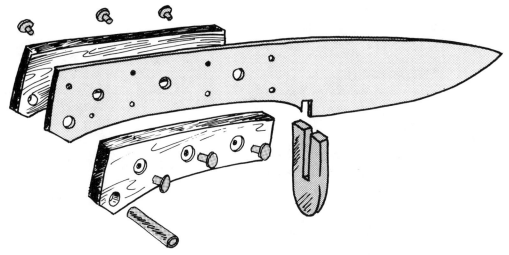

Exploded diagram of full-tang all-purpose knife.

LIST OF MATERIALS

Blade: tool steel; ⅛" x 2" x 9"

Guard: 2 square inches of brass sheet, about ⅛" (8 gauge B&S) thick

Handle slabs: antler, wood, plastic, etc.

Thong tube: brass tube, about ³⁄₁₆" diameter x 1"

Cutlers' rivets: three

Epoxy

Principal Tools: saw, file, drill, vise, heat-treating equipment.

PROCESS OVERVIEW

1. Design the knife and make a full-size drawing.
2. Transfer the drawing onto the steel and cut out the silhouette of the knife.
3. File the edges smooth, refining the outline shape.
4. Drill holes in the tang area. These will be used to rivet on the handle slabs and to assist the glue used to

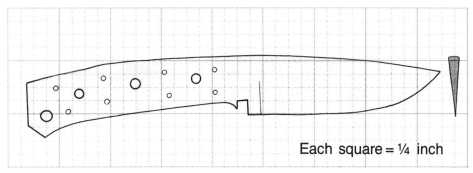

Each square = ¼ inch

Scale drawing of full-tang all-purpose knife.

hold the handle slabs.

5. Define the ricasso and file this area carefully. Once established, file the blade bevel along the rest of the blade. Remove the file marks with coarse, then medium abrasive paper.

6. Harden and temper the steel. Clean the blade with fine abrasive paper (#400).

7. Cut out the brass guard and file it to its final form. It must make a tight fit on the blade.

8. With the guard clamped into position, apply flux and pieces of soft solder. Heat with a torch until the solder flows.

9. Trace the tang shape onto the handle material and cut out the slabs.

10. Drill holes in the handle material to correspond with the larger holes already drilled in the tang.

11. After proper degreasing, spread epoxy onto the tang area and clamp the handle slabs into position, using pins to hold them in alignment.

12. When the glue has hardened, counter-bore holes for the rivet heads. Set the cutlers' rivets.

13. Glue the thong tube into position and gently flare its ends.

14. Finish off the edges of the handle, making them flush with the steel all around. If wooden slabs are used, apply a finishing oil after the final sanding.

15. Sharpen the knife on an oilstone.

DESIGN CONSIDERATIONS

This knife vies with the pocket knife as the most popular of all shapes. As the name says, it is an all-purpose blade, handy on a camping trip, around the yard, in the preparation of food, and in a hundred other ways. It is one of the first knives a person owns, perhaps purchased through the Boy Scouts or in anticipation of a first fishing trip. It should be comfortable, hefty enough to stand up to tough use, and thin enough on the edge to take a sharp bevel.

There are infinite possibilities for the shape of this knife. A few of the traditional shapes are illustrated here. The example being made in this project is a drop point with a sleek modern line.

Here are a few other ideas for a camp or utility knife.

A 9-inch utility knife by Chuck Evans, of 01 steel with a walnut handle. (Photo courtesy of the artist)

PROCESS DETAIL

[1] Probably the best way to get started is to make some quick sketches on paper, making an effort to try out many different ideas. Avoid the trap of getting too attached to an idea right away. I recommend drawing near actual size. When you have laid out as many rough ideas as possible, select a couple favorites and draw variations on these. Continue to narrow down the field until you have reached your final design. Draw this to the actual size you want it. It's a good idea to cut the shape out of cardboard so you can get the feel of it in your hand. When you have decided on the design, draw it full size and transfer the silhouette onto the steel.

As explained in the last chapter, this can be achieved in several ways. The paper pattern can be glued directly onto the steel with a white glue or rubber cement. Another method starts by coating the cleaned piece of steel with a thin layer of quick-drying paint called *Layout Dye*. This alcohol-based paint dries in seconds, which makes it handy, but any spray paint can be used as well. It is important to create only a very thin layer.

The cardboard pattern can then be traced with a scribe, scratching through the paint. The result is a shiny silver-colored line that shows up well. Another method is to draw your pattern onto white contact paper. I use the paper sold by print shops as label stock.

[2] The blade is cut out, using a jeweler's sawframe or, if one is available, a band saw. It is more efficient to go slowly and stay close to your line than to hurry through and "rough out" the form. The time you save by quick sawing will be taken up in refining the form. In the process you will have jeopardized the care spent in laying out the design in the first place.

[3] The blank is then set up in a vise and filed on the edge to refine the shape and remove the marks left by the saw.

[4] Centerpunch and drill holes for the rivets that hold the handle slabs. I have used three holes here, but bear in mind that any number may be used. The rivet will make a bright dot on the handle and is an important part of the design. Its placement is not only a practical matter, but one of aesthetics as well. Don't place the rivets too close to the edge. This risks splitting the handle material or wear-

Cutlers' rivets consist of two pieces with identical heads. The shaft of one is solid, and makes a tight fit into the hollow shaft of the other piece.

ing away the rivet head as the handle is rounded into a comfortable shape. The size of the rivet is similarly a matter of looks. I'm using a ⅜ inch rivet here. This is large and gives the knife a sense of ruggedness. The same size rivet on a more delicate knife would be out of proportion.

Cutlers' Rivets

In this example I'm using a commercial device called *cutlers' rivets*. As shown, these consist of two pieces. One half looks like a nail with a large head and a blunt point. The other half has an identical head, but its shank is a thick-walled tube. The parts are assembled by squeezing them together, forcing the solid part into the tube where a very solid grip is achieved. Cutlers' rivets are available in brass and nickel silver from knifemaking supply companies. A person with jewelrymaking skills can fabricate cutlers'

rivets in other shapes and materials as needed.

In determining the hole size for these rivets, choose a drill bit that is slightly larger than the tube shank. This will allow for the slight swelling that occurs when the two halves are pressed together.

The scale drawing at the beginning of the chapter shows a series of smaller holes all along the tang. These were drilled to provide extra grip for the epoxy that will be used to bond the handle slabs. The placement of these is not critical because they will not be seen when the knife is finished, but it's important to keep them safely away from the edges of the tang.

The large hole closest to the end of the tang is for a thong by which the knife can be hung. Many hobby shops sell brass tube in a range of sizes, usually in lengths of a foot. Buy a piece that is in correct proportion to the rest of the knife and drill a hole that makes a snug fit for it.

Remember that if your drill bit is too small it's possible to enlarge the hole by filing.

[5] The ricasso edge is drawn on and carefully filed. When this and the blade area adjacent to it have been accurately shaped, proceed to the filing of the blade itself. Work on both sides, making certain that an equal amount is being removed from each side. The blade taper should go at least three-fourths of the way up the side of the knife. The last inch or two of the tip should also taper in thickness. Keep in mind that a thinner blade will result in a sharper edge but a more delicate knife.

When the blade taper has reached what seems to be the best shape, remove the file marks with abrasive paper. I recommend silicon carbide paper, which I wrap around a flat stick. This improves leverage and control and extends the life of the paper. Refer to chapter 1 for a description of how to make sanding sticks. Usually the filing is followed by a #100 grit sandpaper. This will be followed in turn by grits #240 and #320. It is important to be sure that each paper has done its job before going onto the next stage. The #100 paper, for example, must remove all the file marks. The #240 then, must remove all the marks made by the #100 paper, and so on. These grit numbers are only suggestions. The difference between, say, a #220 and a #240 is so slight that they may be used interchangeably.

Hardening and Tempering

[6] Harden and temper the blade, as described in the last chapter. Because this blade is larger and thicker than the paring knife, more heat will be needed to bring it to critical temperature. A hand-held propane torch will develop sufficient heat but it may take a while. The process can be hastened by setting up firebricks behind the brick on which the knife blank is set. This wall will reflect the heat back onto the steel. When the blade is a uniform red orange color, quench it quickly in a can of oil (or water if it's a W steel), stirring as you do so.

If hardening by color seems difficult, try this alternate method. When the steel

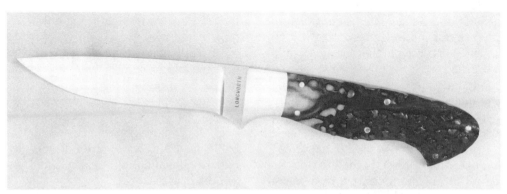

A drop-point camp knife by Dave Longworth. The blade is 4½ inches long and the handle is of stag. Note the delicate effect created by the small rivets. (Photo courtesy of the artist)

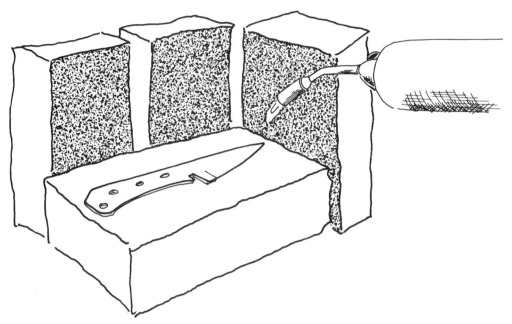

To get the most from a small torch, set up a wall of firebricks to reflect heat back to the workpiece.

undergoes the crystalline change that renders it hard, it loses its magnetism. By quickly touching the steel to a magnet lying on the workbench you will be able to tell if it has achieved the correct heat. Either a steel or a ceramic magnet may be used for this. Be careful to move quickly or the steel will lose heat before you can quench it. If you don't work efficiently, it's possible that the steel could be at the correct temperature when you test it but cool down too much before you quench it.

It's a good habit, before going on to the next step, to test the hardness of the blade by rubbing it with a file. If hardening has been done correctly the file will slip across the blade, making a thin glassy sound. When the blade passes this test, sand it with a medium grit sandpaper (e.g. #320 grit) to remove the black oxide film.

The steel is tempered by carefully heating it to a specific temperature. Commercial heat-treating equipment relies on sophisticated heat sensors, but hand workers usually judge the temperature of the steel through a series of colors that appear as the steel is heated. These are the result of oxides that form on the surface of the metal, and while the oxide layer itself has nothing to do with the property of the steel, it serves as a guide to the temperature inside. It is this temperature change, or more correctly, the crystal changes caused by the increase of heat, that relieves brittleness within the blade. Consult chapter 2 for a more detailed explanation of the science and the goal of heat-treating.

Proper heat-treatment for a blade will have the knife edge heated to a straw yellow color (about 550°F). This color indi-

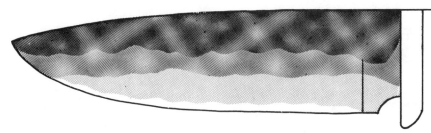

Proper tempering is read through colors created by oxide films of different depths. These accurately reflect crystalline changes within the steel. The cutting edge should be pale straw colored. Immediately behind that is a band of deep straw, followed by a band of plum color. The spine of the knife should be heated to bright blue.

cates maximum edge-holding capability, or resistance to abrasion. It is also the most brittle. The area just behind this will be heated to a plum color (about 600°F), and the rest of the blade will be heated to blue (about 650°F). Notice that the thinnest area of the blade is the part that is to be heated to the lowest temperature. The thin area will heat up first, so some fancy heat control is needed.

One method is to direct the torch flame along the back of the knife. Allow the heat to travel outward from the back (thick area) toward the blade, and halt the flow of heat by quenching the blade as soon as the straw color reaches the edge. This quench can be done in either oil or water.

Another method uses a kitchen stove or hot-plate. Set the blade directly onto the burner of an electric stove so the thick part of the blade lies across the coil. The cutting edge should not be in direct contact with the coil. Use tweezers or pliers to move the blade around on the coil, controlling the flow of colors as they appear.

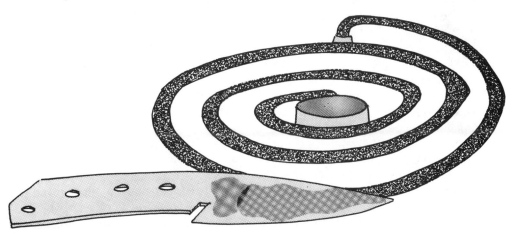

Tempering a blade on a stove or hot-plate. Use pliers or tweezers to move the blade around. In this way it is possible to "paint" with the heat, directing it as needed.

"Cactus Knife" by David Engbritson. This 5¼-inch knife is made of 01 steel with a Micarta handle. (Photo courtesy of the artist)

When the correct colors are reached, remove the blade and quench it if necessary.

It's possible to control the flow of heat so well that the timing of the removal will allow the heat to travel just to where it is wanted and then dissipate. In this case the quench is not necessary. Just removing the blade from the coil (or removing the torch flame) at the right moment will achieve the intended results. Until you have enough experience to accomplish this, though, quench the blade as soon as it reaches the correct temper.

Before going any further it's a good idea to test the temper of the blade. As stated earlier, the goal of tempering is to create a steel that is flexible enough to give under pressure, but tough enough to take and hold an edge. There are many ways to test a blade, some complicated and others simple. The method I use is one of the simpler ones, its advantages being in its ease and immediate results. To test for flexibility, set the tip of the knife on the workbench with the knife held at about a 45-degree angle. Lean on the blade enough to make it bow noticeably. Release the pressure and sight along the blade to be certain that it has returned to straight. There is the remote possibility that the blade could snap off when you bend it. Of course this would be a great disappointment, but it's better to find out now than later. The reason would probably be because of insufficient heat when tempering the blade, but internal stresses in the steel could also cause the blade to break.

To test the toughness of the knife, you'll need a cutting edge. Cut a sharp edge bevel onto one section of the blade with an oilstone or a file. This is not the final edge, so don't bother being too fussy about it. This is only for the purpose of spot-checking your work so far. Using this section of the blade, whittle a large nail or similar piece of mild steel as shown. If the hardening and tempering were done correctly, and assuming that the steel was a tool steel in the first place, the knife should turn up a tiny curl. The blade should show no sign of wear. If all is in order it's time to work on the brass pieces.

[7] The brass guard is cut in the shape of a letter U and made to fit over the tang of the knife. This is easily stated, but will require care in both the laying out and the cutting if the fit is going to be a good one.

And it should be. It is absolutely critical that the fit of the guard to the knife be precise. Any flaws here will not only spoil the looks of the knife but will also greatly undermine the strength of the solder joint. If your first attempt is a poor fit, cut out a new guard. The time is better spent this way than in trying to cover up a sloppy job later on.

File the guard to a comfortable and appealing shape. Follow the use of files with abrasive papers, again going from coarse to fine. A #400 grit paper makes an attractive frosted look that can be considered a final finish. If you want to buff the brass to a mirror finish, continue through even finer papers. It is common practice to have at least the face of the guard, that is, the side that faces the blade of the knife, completely finished before the soldering is done. If the join-

ing is done correctly, all that will be needed to clean that surface after soldering is a cloth.

If you decide on a bright, mirror finish, follow the use of fine abrasive papers with buffing. Before using a buffing machine, refer to chapter 1 for a description of the buffing process. Do not use a buffing machine until you have read this section. There are safety concerns you should know of before starting.

Follow buffing with a thorough washing in soap and ammonia to remove the grease that is a residue of the buffing compound. When the guard is ready, clean the blade area to be soldered with fine abrasive paper or a scouring pad.

Soft Soldering

[8] On this knife we will be joining the

Test the hardness of a blade by cutting into a piece of mild steel like this nail. A properly hardened and tempered blade will turn up a curl without showing any damage to the blade.

A utility knife by Alf Ward in 01 steel, brass, and walnut. Notice how the guard and the rim of the sheath work together. (Photo courtesy of the artist)

guard to the blade with a soft solder. A traditional alloy of tin and lead can be used, but a better choice is an alloy that contains a small amount of silver (around 4%). This is available at some hardware stores and through jewelers' and knife-making supply companies. A couple of popular brand names are Sta-Brite and Tix. The solder is usually sold with its own flux, a clear colorless liquid. Be sure to get this, because without it the solder will not make a proper joint.

With a clean brush or a cotton swab, paint the blade and the inside of the guard with flux. Slide the guard into position and grip it with Vise-Grips or a C-clamp to hold it there. As shown, I set the knife vertically, blade downward. The vise is used only as a holding device. It is not clamped tight enough to mark the blade. The knife could also be set up in a dish of sand or stuck into a board for this operation.

Cut two or three ¼-inch pieces of solder and place them on the guard where it touches the blade. Using more solder will not make a better joint, only a messy one. The trick of good soldering is in a tight fit. Excess solder will not compensate for a sloppy joint.

Gently heat the whole area. Move slowly at first so the rapid boiling of the flux doesn't make the solder flip off. When the flux has stopped bubbling, lower the torch flame to within an inch or so of the knife and continue heating. Move the torch around so the heat is evenly distributed around the whole assembly. As the heat of the knife approaches the flow point of the solder, slightly favor the area below the guard. Because solder flows toward heat, this will "pull" the solder into the joint.

Remove the torch as soon as the solder

has flowed. Most of these solders flow at about 450°F, which is close to the tempering range of the blade. This means it is possible to overheat the knife and disturb the effects created in the tempering process. To avoid doing this, work gingerly and allow the heat time to spread through the steel. Gently "paint" with the torch, using a slow brushing motion over the blade/guard until the solder flows. If the flux smokes and turns black, you have overdone it. Stop immediately and quench the blade in water. Clean off the steel and brass with abrasive paper or a scouring pad to remove the black film that will have formed. Start the soldering operation from the beginning.

When the solder has flowed, allow it about a minute to harden fully. Eagerness in cooling the solder by quenching can result in a brittle joint. When the blade has cooled to the point where it can almost be held in the hand, it is removed from the vise and cooled either in air or water. Check the joint by pulling it hard. When you are satisfied that the solder joint has been well made, the guard can be filed to shape and finished. Take care when doing this that you don't slide a file or sandpaper against the finished areas of the blade.

[9] The handle slabs are prepared by cutting pieces that have a smooth, flat side. Slabs of wood, Micarta, linen Micarta, Pakkawood, antler, and mother-of-pearl are all commercially available. Power sanding machines are very useful in establishing a flat face on each of the slabs, but hand sanding will achieve the same result with a little work.

The first step after getting a flat slab is to file or sand the edge of the slab that will fit against the guard. A precise fit here is one sign of a carefully made knife.

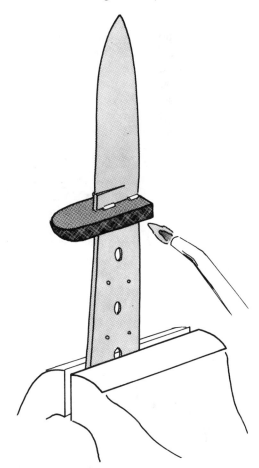

Soldering is done with the blade held vertically. By directing the heat from underneath, solder is pulled into the joint.

Take your time and make the fit perfect. When you are satisfied that this area makes a tight fit, slide a slab into position and with a felt pen trace the outline of the tang. Make a note of which side of the tang this piece is meant for, for instance by marking an X on the slab and on that part of the tang. Repeat the tracing for the other slab. With a band saw, coping saw, or jeweler's saw, cut along this line.

[10] Use Vise-Grips to clamp a slab lightly into position and hold it there while drilling holes. To ensure alignment, drill through the holes in the tang. Remove this piece, flip the knife over, and repeat the process. Haste at this seemingly simple step can ruin a good slab. Take your time and double-check the fit before drilling the hole.

[11] Clean finger oils from the tang area by rubbing it with alcohol, lacquer thinner, or nail polish remover. Mix epoxy glue according to the manufacturer's instructions and spread a thin coat onto both sides of the tang. Lay the handle slabs into position, being certain that the holes line up. Set the whole assembly in a vise and clamp it firmly, but not so hard you risk breaking the slabs. You might want to protect the handle material from being scarred in the vise by cushioning it with paper towel or pieces of leather.

Leave it undisturbed until the glue sets. You might also want to cover the blade or enclose it so a person passing by doesn't accidently get hurt. Read the glue label to check the setting time: it could be from two to twenty-four hours. Don't tempt fate by shortening this time.

[12] When the glue has completely set, remove the knife from the vise and check to see that the holes are clear. Drill them out if they have filled with glue. The cutlers' rivets in this example have been countersunk so they lie flush with the handle. Before preparing the recess that will give this effect, be sure that the two slabs are close to the intended finished thickness. Keep in mind that the slabs are not supported at this stage. Avoid putting stress on the assembly. Use files, rasps, or a sanding machine to establish roughly the shape of the handles. Recesses are then cut to fit the rivet heads.

Making a Spade Bit

The measurements for the diameter and depth of this hole are taken from the head of the rivets being used. A store-bought drill bit can be used to make this countersinking cut, but I've found it just as easy to make my own bit.

Start with a large common nail or a 4-inch length of ³⁄₁₆-inch welding rod. Because this tool will be used only on soft material, it does not need to be hardened and tempered. As shown in the drawing, flatten about an inch at one end by hitting it with a hammer. File the shape shown in the illustration. The

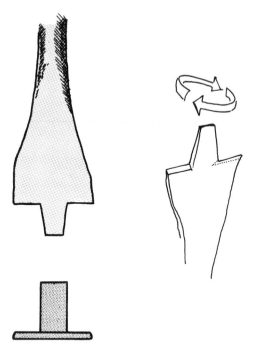

A spade bit improvised from a large nail. This is used to set the heads of the cutlers' rivets flush with the handle.

small projecting tip is the same size as the rivet hole drilled through the wood. Its function is to guide the larger part of the bit. The larger part is as broad as the diameter of the rivet head. Make this bit by first roughing out the shapes with a file. Set the improvised bit into a drill and, with the machine running, hold a file against the bit to complete the shaping. This guarantees that the cutting edges are symmetrical and in line with the axis of the bit. The two edges that reach from the guide pin to the outside of the bit are the cutting edges. These are filed at an angle that slants away from the direction of rotation. As the bit is being shaped, make repeated trials in a piece of scrap wood.

When the bit can consistently cut a recess that perfectly fits the heads of the cutlers' rivets, use it to counter-bore the top part of each rivet hole. Remember not to cut the thong hole.

When the holes are prepared, the rivets

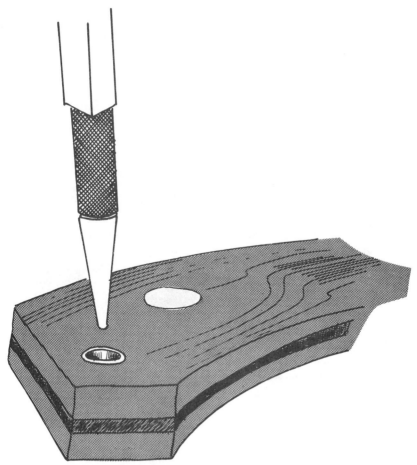

To lodge the brass tube in place for a thong, use a nail set or similarly shaped tool to flare the mouth of the tubing outward.

can be set into place. Unless your handle is exceptionally thick or thin the rivets are probably ready to use. When the rivet halves are squeezed together, their total length will be the length of the tube half plus the thickness of the two heads. Hold the rivet up beside the handle to be sure it will work. If the handle you're making is very thin, you may have to cut off a short piece of each part of the rivet. If you do this, remember to refile the bevel on the tip of the solid shaft. It is very important in lining up the two pieces.

To improvise a cutlers' rivet for a very thick handle, you'll need two solid pins for every one tube. Cut the head off the hollow unit so you have a short length of tube. This is lightly tapped onto the end of one of the solid pins, then the units are assembled.

One method of squeezing the rivet halves together is by tapping them with a hammer. The knife handle should be supported on a solid surface like an anvil while doing this. Another method is to hold the knife between the jaws of a vise. As it is closed, the slow pressure of the vise will gradually drive the rivet halves together. The result is the same in either case. The heads on the two parts of the cutlers' rivet are identical, so it doesn't matter which piece goes on which side.

[13] The brass tubing is now inserted into the hole nearest the end of the handle. It is held in place by epoxy and by a flaring of the ends of the tube. Cut the tube to a length just slightly longer than the thickness of the handle. With a file or a curl of sandpaper, cut a small bevel around the top edges of the hole. Clean the brass and coat it with epoxy, then slide it into place. The mouth of the tube on each end is flared by pressing a tapered rod into it. A nail set or scribe will work well at this, as shown.

[14] The outer edge of the handle is filed and sanded to become flush with the steel of the tang. The shape of the handle is then refined and rounded with rasps, files, and sandpaper. No sealer is needed on antler, but if wood is used it should be sealed. I used an even mixture of linseed oil and varnish. The mix was liberally rubbed on with a cloth and allowed to soak into the wood for about half an hour. The excess was then wiped off, and the finish was allowed to dry overnight. This process was repeated four times. There are several commercial preparations that will also produce attractive and durable results.

[15] As a last step the blade is honed on an oilstone. See chapter 3 for advice on how to do this.

Even a knife as wonderful as the one you just made won't do you much good it it's home on a shelf when you need it out in the woods. To finish the job you'll want to make a sheath. A sheath for this knife, as well as directions on making it, is illustrated in chapter 4.

8

PROJECT 3:

Partial-Tang Carving Knife

*This simple and straightforward style is popular for
its versatility and light weight. Because the tang
is completely enclosed within the handle, this style lends
itself to continuous handle material and designs.
This project teaches sawing, drilling, filing, silver
soldering, and wood carving.*

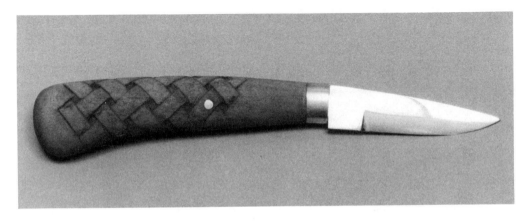

Exploded diagram of partial-tang carving knife.

LIST OF MATERIALS

Blade: tool steel; $\frac{1}{16}'' \times 5'' \times 1''$

Handle: wood, antler, bone, etc.

Ferrule: sterling silver; about 2 square inches of 20-gauge B&S; brass or nickel silver could also be used

Pin: rod of sterling, brass, or nickel silver; $\frac{1}{8}'' \times 1''$

Principal Tools: saw, files, drill, heat-treating equipment, silver solder, abrasive papers, epoxy

PROCESS OVERVIEW

1. Make many sketches and choose your favorites. Draw them full-size on heavy cardboard. Cut these out and test the design for size and a comfortable feel in the hand.
2. Lay out the blade shape on steel. Drill the hole.
3. Saw out the blade shape. File its outline to smooth away saw marks.
4. File the blade taper in the steel, giving special attention to the ricasso area.
5. Heat-treat the blade.
6. Finish the steel to at least a #400 grit abrasive paper. Buff if desired.
7. Prepare handle slabs by cutting the wood to size and sanding two faces perfectly flat.
8. Carve a recess in each slab for the tang. Drill a hole in each.

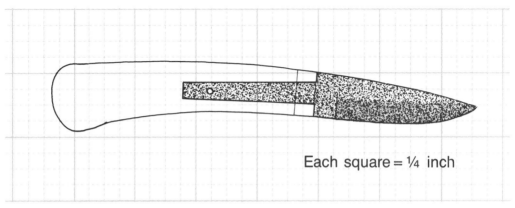

Each square = ¼ inch

Scale drawing of partial-tang carving knife.

9. Glue the handle halves together.
10. Shape the handle with rasps, files, sanding machine, etc.
11. Make a ferrule and fit it to the handle or carve the handle and make a ferrule to fit that. Finish to taste.
12. Carve the handle (optional).
13. Test fit. Assemble the pieces, using epoxy.
14. Set the pin with glue and rivet the ends lightly.
15. Hone.

DESIGN CONSIDERATIONS

This knife is considered a simple construction that economizes on materials. Because little steel is used, the knife is lightweight. This makes it easy to manipulate, which is why it is popular for carving. Because the tang is enclosed, this style invites designs that work their way completely around the handle. This is illustrated in the project shown here. The maple handle is carved in a pattern that surrounds the grip.

The ferrule in this example is made of sterling silver and gives the knife not only a literal but an aesthetic worth. Other metals could be used and of course the metal could be decorated in a variety of ways. Knifemakers familiar with jewelrymaking skills will immediately perceive the wide range of effects that could be used to advantage in this piece.

When you lay out the handle, consider the effect of leverage on the tang. Be sure to leave sufficient material to protect the end of the tang. In the case of bone or antler where the inside might be soft, it is possible to make a metal sleeve to fit into and reinforce this area. Because the tang will be slid into the handle, it should taper slightly from the blade (the widest area) to the tip.

In this project, the partial-tang style is illustrated in a carving knife. This class of knives is characterized by a thin, short blade and a handle that fits easily into the hand. The partial-tang method of construction can, of course, be used on many other kinds of knives. Important examples are traditional Japanese knives and swords, which are almost all assembled in this way.

Carving knives are known for their short blades and comfortable handles. Here are a few more ideas.

PROCESS DETAIL

[1] As before, start by sketching many ideas. Aim for a form that achieves a harmonious union of the blade, ferrule, and handle. Avoid getting attached to a single idea too soon. By starting with many diverse ideas you will have the widest possible selection from which to choose.

Select a couple of your favorite designs and draw these to actual size on heavy cardboard. Cut these out and roll each around in your hand to get the feel of the finished knife. Is it comfortable? Does it fall into your grip in a natural, ready-to-use position? Are there sharp corners that will fatigue the hand during long use? Make any modifications that these reflections indicate, and if the changes are radical, cut a new template. Time spent in this early stage will give increased pleasure and confidence through the rest of the knifemaking.

When the silhouette of the knife has been decided, draw it onto the template to determine the size and shape of the ferrule and the blade. Copy the blade shape onto label paper and stick it onto the steel.

[2] Centerpunch and drill the hole in the tang. Doing this before cutting out the blade provides a large piece of steel to hold onto. This makes the drilling safer. The size of this hole is not critical except that it must match perfectly the pin that will secure the blade into the handle. In this example the hole is 1/16 inch.

Sawing and Filing

[3] The blade can be sawn out with a jeweler's saw, a band saw or a hacksaw.

[4] File the bevel into the blade. Because this knife is to be delicate and lightweight, the first step in shaping the blade is to thin the steel toward the point. Draw and file the ricasso lines. Grind/file the blade until a thin, sharp edge is all that remains. Remove the file marks with coarse abrasive paper. Continue sanding with increasingly finer abrasives until reaching a grit in the 300s.

Hardening and Tempering

[5] Harden the blade by heating it to a bright red orange and quenching it in oil. The tang can be left unhardened. Use

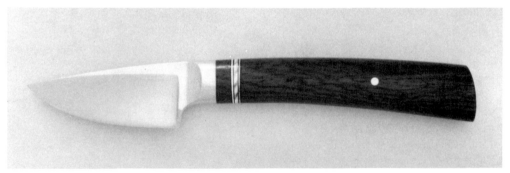

A dropped-edge utility knife by David Boye. The decorative band near the blade is made of two contrasting metals. (Photo courtesy of the artist)

Five cast-forged blades with decorative rings by David Boye. (Photo courtesy of the artist)

the same #300 grit paper just mentioned to remove the black oxide scale. This is done to reveal the color changes of tempering more clearly. Heat the steel slowly, bringing the whole blade to a plum color. The carving stroke for which this knife is intended will put a sideways pressure against the blade, so it is important to relieve brittleness. This is the reason the whole blade is taken to the plum color. Of course this sacrifices a small amount of edge-holding potential in the steel.

[6] Finish the blade as desired. A #400 grit abrasive paper will give a bright frosted look; a #500 grit will create a dull shine; and a #600 paper will make a bright silver-colored appearance. For a mirrorlike finish, use a hand buff or a buffing wheel. See chapter 1 for details.

Preparing the Handle Slabs

[7] Prepare the handle slabs by cutting two rectangles of wood about ⅜ inch thick and slightly larger than the intended handle. I like to leave the wood in a rectangular shape as long as possible. This makes it easier to grip the slabs in a vise.

Sand the two faces of the wood that will be joined. By paying attention to the grain of the wood you should be able to find patterns that can be joined almost invisibly.

[8] Set one of the slabs in a vise or clamp it onto a table with the sanded side facing up. Lay the finished blade on it and trace the tang with a sharp pencil. This area will be carved away to a depth of half the thickness of the steel. If you

With the handle block set into the vise, carve a recess equal in depth to half the blade thickness.

are using ¹⁄₁₆-inch steel this is only ¹⁄₃₂ inch so don't get carried away.

The carving can be done with wood-carving chisels, a utility knife, linoleum carving tools, or gravers. If you don't have the right tool you can make one. You are a knifemaker, after all. The photograph shows a couple tools made to fill this need. One is a dull needle file that was broken off at the tip and honed on an oilstone. Because the file was already hard, no heat treatment was necessary. The tool next to it was made from a scrap of blade steel. It is obvious that no time was spent in shaping the stock. I simply took a likely looking scrap, filed a bevel on one end, and heat-treated the tip. The whole process took less than five minutes. Next to that is a slightly more refined version of the same tool. In this case I took the time to file the scrap to a straight bar and after filing a point onto

the back end I drove this into an old file handle. This one probably took ten minutes. The point is that you don't need to get too fancy about the tool you use to carve this recess.

Check the recess periodically as the carving proceeds. A snug fit is necessary for a sturdy knife. If you accidentally carve too deep with a stroke or two, the irregularity can be overlooked. If the whole carving is too deep, sand the block until the proper depth is achieved. Lay the tang back into place and use a sharp pencil to mark the location of the hole. Drill it.

Repeat the process on the other slab. Set the two pieces together and slide the blade into position. If there is a snag, separate the halves and correct the problem.

[9] Use a white glue (such as Elmer's) to bond the handle slabs together. Apply the glue sparingly and be careful that it

doesn't spill over into the recess. Line up the halves carefully and clamp them together in C-clamps, a vise, or Vise-Grips. It is important that the halves line up perfectly or the tang won't slide into position. Sometimes by sighting into the recess it is possible to line up the halves. To be especially cautious, set up and clamp the handle pieces with the tang in place, then slide it out before the glue dries. Resist the temptation to coat the tang with a wax or oil before setting it in. It's true that this will prevent the glue from grabbing onto the steel, but later when the knife is being assembled for real this would prevent a tight bond.

[10] When the glue has set, the handle is removed from its clamps and the hole is checked to be sure it is still open. If it has filled in, drill it out now. The next step is to cut the handle to its final shape. Trace the original cardboard template onto the wood and use a saw to cut away as much excess material as you can. The form is then defined by filing and sand-ing. Check the feel of the knife periodically to guarantee that it is a comfortable shape. Finish with increasingly finer grades of sandpaper. Use flint or aluminum oxide papers (made for wood) rather than the silicon carbide papers used on metal.

Making the Ferrule

[11] The next step is to make the ferrule. This can be approached in a couple ways. Either carve the wood to the intended shape and make the ferrule to fit it, or reverse the sequence. Make the ferrule to a prescribed shape, then carve the wood to fit into it. The end result will be the same; the choice has to do with your skills as a metalsmith and the design of your knife. In my case I wanted the ferrule to be a symmetrical oval, so I started by making the ferrule to the shape I wanted and then cut the wood until the cap slipped into place.

I used an oval template to determine

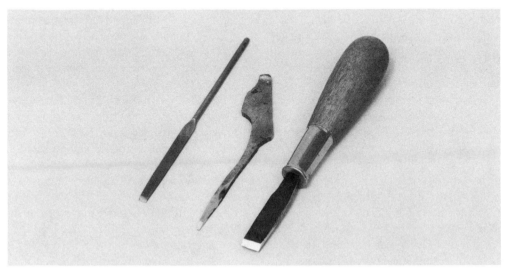

Carving tools can be improvised from any scrap of tool steel.

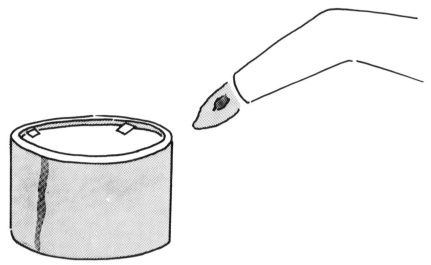

The ferrule is set on a soldering block and fluxed. Set a couple small pieces of solder into position and heat gently with a torch until they flow.

the size and shape of the oval I needed. Another method is to fold a paper into fourths and cut it to make a symmetrical oval. This shape was scribed onto a sterling sheet and sawn out. I used a strip of paper to help estimate the length needed to wrap around this oval, then cut out a strip of sterling that was a little longer than I estimated. I made the ferrule about ½ inch high but it could have been either larger or smaller.

Using pliers, wrap the strip around the oval and mark it where it makes a good fit. Cut the strip at this point, file the ends until they fit together neatly, then solder this seam. Use silver (hard) solder and an appropriate flux such as Handy Flux. Do not use a lead-base solder, because the result would not stand up to the forming that comes next.

At this point the strip is an irregular loop. To give it a regular form, shape it with pliers or by pressing it over a tapered steel rod called a mandrel. This is the point where a lead-soldered joint would probably break. The strip is shaped so the previously cut oval can be fitted into it. Make sure this fit is very snug so the parts stay together for soldering without needing to be propped into position.

Paint the joint around the oval with flux and set several small pieces of silver solder into position at regular intervals around the oval. Apply heat evenly to the whole unit with a torch until the solder flows. File away any traces of solder and any irregularities. Sand the ferrule with increasingly finer grits of silicon carbide abrasive paper, up to #600. At this point the silver can be considered finished. It could also be buffed, either by hand or on a machine, to achieve a mirror polish. Whittle the handle around its top until the ferrule makes a snug fit over it. I used both carving knives and files to achieve this.

[12] As mentioned, the handle can be ornamentally carved. Start by sketching various ideas on paper before deciding which pattern you want on the handle. Once you've decided, draw onto the wood with a pencil to lay out the design. The pattern is cut with the same tools used earlier to carve the recess for the tang. Finish the carving by resanding with a fine grit of abrasive paper. Treat the wood by staining, oiling, and/or waxing it. In this case I applied several coats of the varnish and oil mixture described in the last project.

[13] Test-fit the pieces of the knife together. If all is well, mix up a quantity of epoxy and work a generous amount down into the recess in the wooden handle. Spread some around the inside of the ferrule and slide the pieces together. Re-move any excess glue with a tissue. Be aware that it is possible for the parts to slide apart because of trapped air pressed into the recess during assembly. To prevent this, slide the pin into place. By pulling it back and forth and twisting it, the pin will pick up a coating of epoxy sufficient to hold it in place.

[14] After the glue has dried, use a saw or snips to cut the pin to a length extending only slightly out of the handle. File both ends of the pin flat. Set the pin on an anvil or similar steel surface and tap each end alternately with a hammer to flare it.

[15] The blade is sharpened on an oilstone as explained in chapter 3.

The result is a handsome and practical knife, a personal tool that will give many years of kindly service.

9

PROJECT 4:

Through-Tang Skinner

This multipurpose knife can be made in a variety of sizes and materials. The important difference between this knife and the knife shown in Project 2 is the method of construction. In this knife the tang is a narrow shaft that extends through the handle and out the end, where it is threaded. The handle assembly is held onto the blade by a nut or threaded cap screwed onto the back end of the knife.
This chapter teaches threading, stamping, and the use of antler.

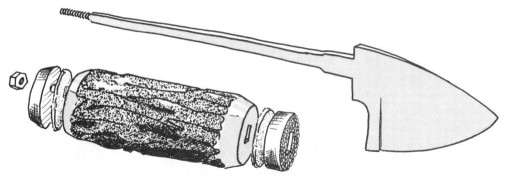

Exploded diagram of through-tang skinner.

LIST OF MATERIALS

Blade: tool steel, roughly ³⁄₁₆" x 2" x 9"

Guard: about 4 square inches of brass or nickel silver sheet at least ⅛" thick

Handle: wood, antler, horn, plastic, etc.

Principal Tools: saw, files, drill, a threading die, heat-treating equipment, finishing equipment

PROCESS OVERVIEW

1. Create a design and draw a full-size plan. Refer to the figure for the shape of the tang.

2. Saw the blade shape from a piece of tool steel.

3. File or grind the blade to the desired bevel; finish to #300 grit. Add file decoration to the spine edge if desired.

4. Heat-treat the blade, then finish to #400 grit.

5. File the last half-inch of the tang into a round cross-section.

6. Cut threads in this area with a die.

7. From brass sheet, cut the pieces to be used for the guard and the end cap. Drill a hole in each and cut the

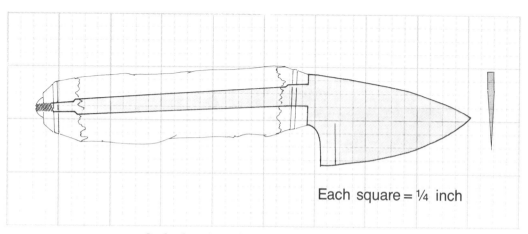

Each square = ¼ inch

Scale drawing of through-tang skinner.

guard hole to a rectangular shape. It must make a snug fit over the tang and a close fit against the shoulder of the blade.

8. Cut the material to be used as a handle and drill a hole through the center. Use a modified rasp to alter this hole from a round to a rectangular shape. Prepare any other sections to be used in the handle, seeing that each has a rectangular hole. Assemble the handle pieces and check the fit.

9. Restack the pieces, this time with a layer of epoxy between each layer.

10. Screw the end nut up tight and allow the glue to set.

11. File or grind the handle to its final shape, progressing through increasingly finer grits to #500. Apply the desired finish.

DESIGN CONSIDERATIONS

The advantage of this style of construction over the full tang shown earlier has to do with the different look in the handle. The full-tang knife must show a line of steel on the handle. This method allows the handle to be a complete unit that surrounds and encloses the tang. Materials such as antler, horn, and some configurations of wood particularly lend themselves to the through-tang handle.

In this example, spacers of leather have been used. Plastic, wood, metal, or other materials can be included to enhance the design. Another popular use of this style uses disks of leather stacked one on top of the next to create an attractive and durable handle. A through-tang knife with a leather handle is illustrated in project 6.

The short, broad curving blade illustrated here is called a skinner. Besides its use in dressing game, the shape makes a handy chopping blade for the kitchen. The size and shape of the blade used in a through-tang knife have no limitation. The only guidelines are the maker's ideas and the uses for which the knife is intended.

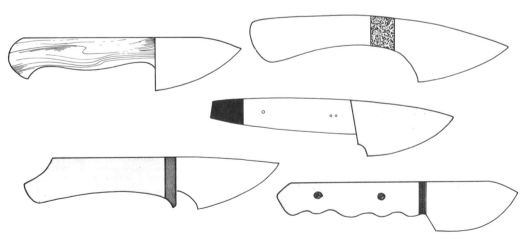

A skinner is characterized by a short broad blade with a sweeping curve. Here are a few examples to trigger your imagination.

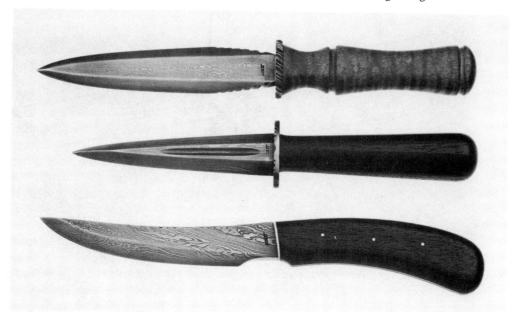

Three blades by Scott Lankton with handles by P. S. Diem. The top is a boot knife with a maple handle, the middle example is a flat-backed boot knife with a blackwood and paduck handle. The bottom is an upswept hunter with a rosewood and ivory handle. (Photo by Weyer of Toledo)

PROCESS DETAIL

[1] Again I recommend starting with many designs, rendered as quick sketches on paper. After a favorite shape has been selected, draw it to actual size. Details are fine-tuned, resulting in a full-scale blueprint. This is transferred to contact paper, which is then pasted onto the blade steel. Remember to clean the steel with sandpaper or a scouring pad to remove its oily skin before adhering the contact paper.

[2] Saw out the blade with either a band saw or a jeweler's saw. You might have to make several entrance cuts, removing the waste areas around the blade in several pieces. Don't be afraid to make these extra cuts. It's often faster and more economical to go about it this way than to labor at turning corners and preserving every possible square inch of steel.

[3] The bevel is filed or ground on the blade. This is done as before, using a power sander, hand files, or a combination of both. As explained in preceding chapters, thought should be given to the ricasso edge. If it is to be sharp I recommend cutting this edge first with a hand file. You can use a piece of scrap steel clamped onto the knife blank to serve as a guide. Set the knife blank into a vise or clamp it into Vise-Grips and set these into a vise. Use other clamps to secure a bar of scrap steel along the line of the ricasso as shown. This assembly is awkward-looking and can take a few minutes to set up, but the resulting sharp edges and efficient filing are worth the trouble.

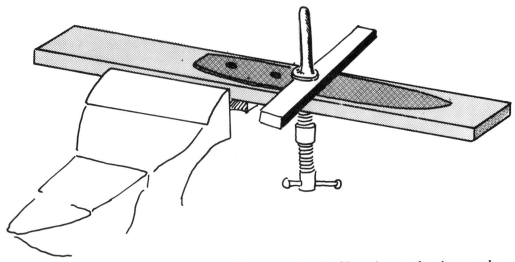

A scrap of steel bar is clamped into position to guide the file as it cuts the ricasso edge.

It is important that an equal amount of metal be removed from each side of the blade so that the cutting edge will be directly on the center of the thickness. A centerline can be drawn with a fine line marker or scratched with a sharp point. Remember to make this reference point before starting to file or grind the blade bevel.

The blade is shaped with hand files or a power sander. Alter the direction of strokes as you progress from one tool or grit of abrasive to the next. Continue in a methodical progression from one coarseness to the next until the blade is finished to around a #300 grit.

File Work Decoration

An attractive detail can be added to the spine edge by filing. Use small files, called *needle files*, and the jeweler's saw to make a pattern. The sample plate illustrated shows a few simple patterns. Go further by inventing your own. The filing

is easily done and moves along quickly. I recommend making some experiments on a piece of scrap steel before working on the knife blade.

Hardening and Tempering

[4] Heat-treat as before. The first step is to harden the blade. Heat it to a bright red orange and quench it in the proper medium (usually oil or water). The tang is left untreated, but it is important to avoid an abrupt change in the temper of the steel just at the point where the blade meets the tang. When heating the blade, allow the red color to move slightly into the tang.

The second step is to temper the steel to achieve the desired combination of flexibility and edge-holding resilience. The body of the blade should be heated to a bright blue color. Along the edge there should be a band of straw yellow about ⅛ inch wide. Between this and the

Small files and the jeweler's saw can be used to create a variety of patterns along edges. This sampler plate shows only a few of the endless possibilities.

blue there should be a band of brownish plum color about ¼ inch wide.

One way to achieve this range of heat is to set the blade on a firebrick so the spine (the thickest part) hangs over the edge. Set a small bar of scrap steel, such as an old file, along the cutting edge to act as a heat sink. Direct a medium torch flame at the brick just under the over-hanging spine of the blade. The brick will soon glow red. In this way, heat is de-flected up against the thick part of the blade. This slows down the flow of heat

and gives it time to spread throughout the blade. The old file laid along the edge will draw heat away from this thin area and protect it from overheating. It's possible to manipulate the pieces and the direc-tion and intensity of the flame. After a few tries you'll find that this arrange-ment offers great flexibility and control. It can be used to temper just about any size and shape of blade. Temper the tang near the blade to blue. Finish the blade to about a #400 grit.

A blade is tempered over a torch flame as shown. More heat flows to the thick part of the blade, which overhangs the brick. The thin cutting edge could be further pro-tected by setting a scrap of steel on it, or by building up a layer of clay on it.

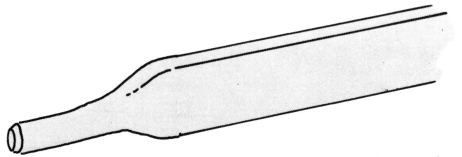

Prepare the end of the tang for threading by filing it to a round cross-section.

Preparing the Tang

[5] In this example the handle is going to be held onto the knife by a nut screwed onto the end of the tang. The first step toward preparing the tang is to make sure that the length of the tang is comfortable in the hand and visually appropriate for the size of the blade. If it is too long, now is the time to cut it off. Proceed slowly so you don't make the mistake of cutting off too much.

File the last inch or so of the tang to a round cross-section as shown. This is the area that will hold the nut. At the end of this cylindrical section, file a slight bevel to facilitate the thread-cutting operation that comes next.

[6] Threads are cut with a small tool called a *threading die*. These steel disks are sold in sets or can be bought individually, usually for less than a dollar a piece. Unless you foresee other uses for threading, I'd recommend buying a single die and a brass or stainless steel nut of the same cut. Thread sizes are given as two numbers; the first refers to the diameter of the shaft and the second to the number of threads per inch. Choose the size that is in proportion to the knife you're making, probably something around a ⅛- or ³⁄₁₆-inch diameter. You

might want to buy a handle to grip the die, but you can economize here by using a pair of Vise-Grips.

To cut the threads, set the knife vertically in a vise with the tip of the blade pointing down. Set the die onto the end of the tang and screw it onto the tang about a half turn. Try to keep the die

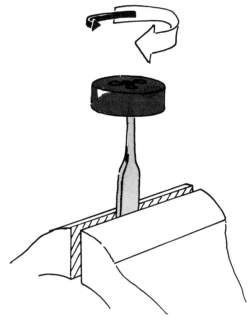

A threading die is used in a screwing-unscrewing motion.

level. Back off (unscrew) a quarter turn to clear away any chips of steel that have been cut. Screw the die again, another half turn. Back off a quarter turn, and squirt a couple drops of oil onto the tang. Continue this screwing-unscrewing motion until you have cut threads along most of the rounded part of the tang. If it is very difficult to turn the die, it may be because the round shaft of the tang is too large for the die you are using. Reduce its diameter by filing and try again.

[7] From a thick brass sheet cut the pieces to be used for the guard and the end cap. Choose a drill bit the same size as the thickness of the tang, or just a little bit smaller. Drill a hole in both the end cap and the guard. Insert a saw blade into the piece that is to be the guard. Fix it into a frame and cut a rectangular hole. This piece must make a snug fit over the tang and a close fit against the shoulder of the blade. It's probably best to cut this hole a little on the small side, then rely on filing to gradually bring it to a perfect fit. Sloppiness here will detract from the effect of the knife.

In this example I have textured the front-facing surface of the guard by making a series of punched circles. The pattern, called "fish roe" by the Japanese, was made with a carpenter's nail set. This is a common tool that is available from any hardware store. The disk of brass should be set onto an anvil or the table of a vise during the hammering. Of course many other textures could be used, or the surface could be left smooth.

Making a Hole in the Antler

[8] Attention can now be given to the handle material. In some cases, such as antler, the piece is simply cut to the right length. Other materials, like wood, might require milling and exterior shaping as well.

The hole that runs down the center must be rectangular, fitting snugly onto the tang. This prevents the handle from

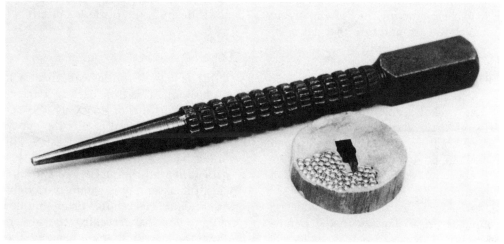

A carpenter's nail set was used to stamp a pebbled pattern on the guard.

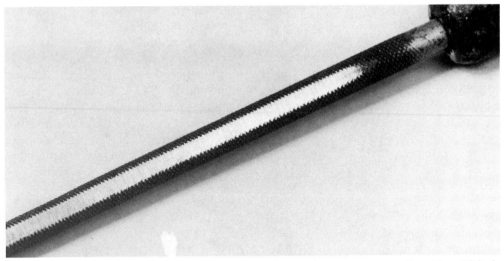

A rasp has been modified by grinding away the teeth on two opposite sides. This is useful in cutting away the bridge of metal between two drilled holes.

rotating. To achieve the rectangular opening, drill a pair of holes, one above the other. The little bridge of material between the holes can be cut away either with a rasp or a chisel, or sometimes by burning with a red-hot piece of scrap steel. (If you've ever smelled burning antler, you'll know that this is a quick way to clear a room.) The accompanying photo shows a round rasp that has been modified for this operation. Use a grinding wheel to remove part of the rasp, leaving a bar with teeth on two sides. This is effective in cutting away the bridge between two holes. Another approach is to drill one hole and file it out from the top and bottom until it is large enough to accommodate the tang. The modified rasp also works well for this kind of enlarging.

In the example shown I've added a couple layers of leather to the handle assembly. These will act as shock absorbers for the antler and will help adjust for any irregularity in the fit. Knifemaking supply companies sell a fibrous material in several colors that could also be used here. The knife made in Project 6 uses this spacer material.

Slide the pieces of the handle into position for a trial run. If everything is in order, the handle pieces are taken off and, if desired, the blade is buffed.

Assembly

[9] The handle pieces are slid back into position. This time each section receives a thin film of epoxy as it is set into place. Be careful to mix the epoxy thoroughly, stirring for at least a full minute.

[10] When all the pieces are slid into place, the assembly is clamped up tight with the nut. Tighten this firmly but not so tight you risk cracking the antler. Allow the epoxy to cure. Follow the manufacturer's instructions carefully.

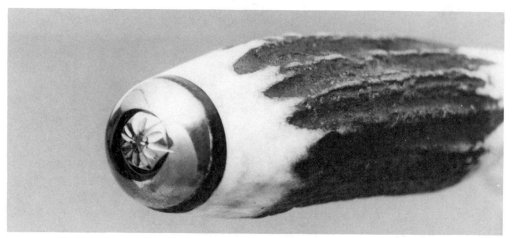

To decorate the butt of this knife, the brass nut was rounded off and scored with some simple file strokes.

[11] When the glue has hardened, the handle can be given its final shape, using files and sandpaper. The heat of grinding, even rapid hand filing, can burn the epoxy and cause it to fail. I recommend holding the knife in bare hands rather than gloves so you will be aware of heat as it accumulates. It's a wiser practice to go slowly, pausing as you work, than to ruin your work by hurrying.

The nut can be left as is, or, with a little ingenuity and some careful filing, be made into a decorative finial like the one shown. Antler is usually left untreated but may be given a light coat of wax if desired. Wood can be finished with linseed oil, commercial oils, varnish, and/or wax.

If the blade was given a high shine before, it might need a touching up on the buffing wheel at this stage. The edge can be honed and stropped. To make a sheath for this knife refer to chapter 4.

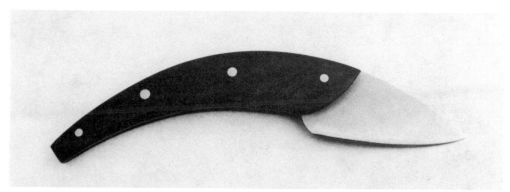

This skinner/utility knife by Chuck Evans is made of 01 steel, with walnut slabs and brass rivets. (Photo courtesy of the artist)

10

PROJECT 5:

Wilderness Knife

This specialty knife is sometimes called a survival knife. It features a hollow handle that can be used to hold supplies needed in the wilderness, such as fishhooks, string, water-purification tablets, and so on. The blade includes a section that is a saw, and the guard has holes that will allow the knife to be mounted onto a shaft as a spear.
This project teaches silver soldering and a new use for commercial pipe fittings.

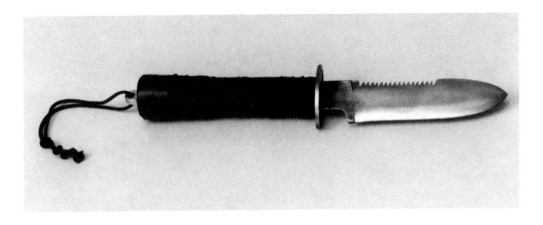

Exploded diagram of wilderness knife.

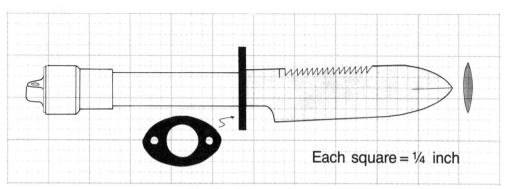

Each square = ¼ inch

Scale drawing of wilderness knife.

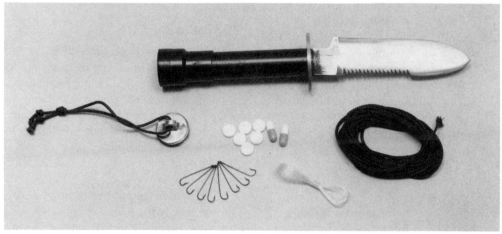

The hollow handle of this knife can be used to carry an assortment of equipment that might be needed in the wild.

LIST OF MATERIALS

Blade: tool steel, about ³⁄₁₆ x 1½" x 8"

Guard: about 3 square inches of thick brass sheet

Handle: 6" piece of copper, brass or stainless steel pipe

Butt: brass plug and threaded fitting

Miscellaneous: 20 feet of heavy cord, fish-hooks, string, small compass, needle and thread, waterproof matches, etc.

Principal Tools: saw, files, soldering and heat-treating equipment

PROCESS OVERVIEW

1. Design the knife and acquire the components. Draw the blade shape onto label paper.
2. Saw out the blade. File its outline to remove file marks and refine the shape. The tang should make a tight fit into the handle.
3. Hard-solder the pipe fitting onto the pipe.
4. Cut away some of the plug to minimize weight. Saw/grind the peg on the plug to an attractive shape. Drill a hole for a thong.
5. Saw out the guard, including thong holes and the central hole for the handle. File as needed until the guard makes a snug fit over the pipe.
6. Hard-solder two half-circles of brass onto the tang area of the blade. File this assembly until it makes a snug fit into the pipe.
7. Heat-treat the blade.
8. Solder the blade into the handle.
9. Apply the final finish as desired. Wrap cord around the handle.
10. Sharpen on an oilstone.

DESIGN CONSIDERATIONS

Of all the projects in this book I think this knife looks the most lethal. It is a no-nonsense tool whose aesthetics depend directly on function and ruggedness. Many commercial knife companies have recently added this style to their product line. One of the popular variations uses a molded plastic handle with a compass set into the inside of the cap. The original models used a stainless steel pipe for the handle. Either of these are first-rate choices and are more sophisticated than the example being made here. The starting point for this knife is somewhat unique. Is it possible, I asked myself, to make this style of knife from common, easily available materials?

This chapter is my answer, and as you can see the answer is yes. If a person has access to a machine shop and can make the parts from stainless steel or similar stock, I'd encourage it. But this knife, as described here, is a hard-working practical knife that can be a pleasure to make and use.

PROCESS DETAIL

[1] The blade shown has a double edge and a saw but any shape of blade could be used. Double-edged blades are illegal in some states, so you might want to check with a law enforcement authority before spending too much time on a design. Start by sketching several variations and choosing the one that appeals to you.

A trip to a plumbing supply house should supply the necessary hardware. In this case I used a 6-inch length of ¾-inch copper pipe, a ¾-inch brass threaded coupling, and a brass internal plug. I found several other fittings that were similar. I suggest having the plumbing components on hand before cutting out the blade. In this way you can be careful to keep the handle and the blade in proportion.

Cut out a cardboard blade and fit it into the handle to try out the shape and size. When the parts seem to go together, trace the blade pattern onto label paper and transfer it to the steel. For this knife I used 440C, but any hardenable steel could be used.

Cutting Out the Blade

[2] Saw out the blade with a band saw or jeweler's saw, as explained previously. Use files or a sanding machine, or both, to refine the outline of the blade. When the silhouette is accurate, grind or file the blade bevel. Remove the coarse marks of rough filing and grinding with increasingly finer abrasives until the blade is a uniform frosted finish.

Pay particular attention to the tang. It must make a tight fit into the handle. Be especially careful not to file away too much here, because this would greatly diminish the strength of the knife.

About midway in the blade-shaping process, stop to cut the saw teeth if they are part of your design. This can be done with a jeweler's saw, a hacksaw, or a file. Note the angle of the teeth in the drawing. This allows cutting on the push stroke, which has more power.

Preparing the Handle

[3] Clean the outside of the copper pipe and the inside of the unthreaded part of the fitting with a scouring pad in preparation for soldering. Though soft solder can be used, I prefer the strength of hard (silver) solder. Apply a generous amount of a brazing flux (such as Handy Flux) and slide the pieces together. Set several small pieces of solder along the joint and begin by heating slowly.

The first step is to evaporate the water from the flux. Bringing the torch close to the metal too soon will only cause a boiling that will throw off the pieces of

Standard plumbing fittings are used for the handle of this knife.

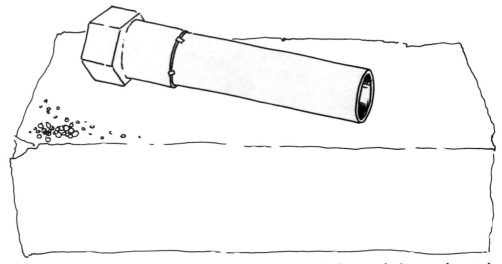

Silver solder the fittings together. Brass, copper, or stainless-steel pipe can be used.

solder. When the flux has stopped bubbling, the torch is brought closer to the metal. Slowly move it along the length of the copper pipe. Use color as a guide to ensure that the two units being soldered (the pipe and the fitting) are about the same temperature at the same time. Heat just until the solder flows, then remove the torch and allow the handle to cool for about half a minute. To dissolve the flux residue, you can clean the metal in a mild pickle, such as the commercial preparation called Sparex, or rinse it in hot running water.

[4] The plug that will become the top of the handle was engineered for ruggedness and ease of manufacture. It doesn't look much like a component for a fine knife. Use a saw, file, or grinder to remove some of the square block. When the remaining tab approaches a more comely size and shape, drill it to accept a thong. In this case I went through the sequence of abrasive papers to a high number like 500, then buffed the brass

to a bright shine. Of course you can stop anywhere along the process that leaves a finish that appeals to you.

[5] Lay out and saw the guard from heavy brass sheet. In this example I followed the standard shape for this style of knife and made an oval. This has about ¾ inch of guard projecting from either side of the knife. I have included two ⅛-inch holes in this section to make it possible to tie the blade onto a pole for use as a spear. Take special care in cutting and filing the large round hole so that it makes a snug fit over the outside of the pipe.

[6] Use a compass or circle template to determine the size of half-circle that, when added to the thickness of the tang, will fill up the handle. Cut two of these from the same stock as the guard. To allow for later filing and fitting, cut them slightly oversize. Use medium or hard silver solder to attach these to the tang. Repeat the steps outlined above for soldering the fitting onto the pipe. Soft (lead-

based) solder can be used for this operation but the knife won't be quite as strong. If soft solder is to be used, delay this step until after the blade has been heat-treated.

Hardening and Tempering

[7] The blade is hardened by heating to a bright red orange. The ricasso and tang are left unheated. Heat the steel to a bright red color and quench it in oil or water as recommended for the steel being used. Test the hardness by rubbing a file along the blade. You should hear a high-pitched, glassy sound. If the hardening is successful, proceed immediately to the tempering. If the blade didn't pass the file test, go back a step and reharden by heating to bright red.

Sand off the black scale on both sides. This will make it easier to "read" the tempering colors. This blade is designed to function in a variety of situations. It might be called on to slice, chop, pry, or saw. Its ability to hold a shaving edge is not as important as its ruggedness, so in this case I will temper to an all-over plum or bluish-purple color. This should create enough flexibility to stand up to rough use without sacrificing too much edge-holding power. Halt the tempering either by quenching or by removing the torch at the appropriate time so the heat never goes past the intended color.

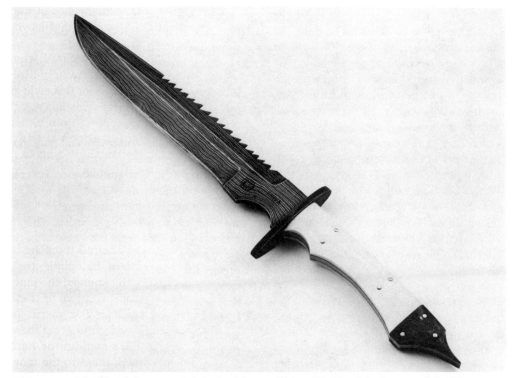

This rugged knife with saw teeth is by Master Shiva Ki. The blade, guard and butt cap are all made of Damascus steel. The handle is ivory. (Photo courtesy of the artist)

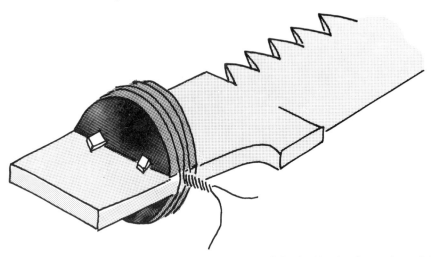

Half-circles of brass are hard-soldered onto the tang of the knife. As shown here, binding wire can be used to hold them in position for soldering.

Assembly

[8] The blade is now forced into the handle and soldered there. This might take some careful filing at the tang. The fit must be snug. The best joint uses silver solder but this will be a little tricky. In order to preserve the temper, the joint must be made with a very hot, very localized flame. A jeweler's oxygen torch or a standard oxy-acetylene welding torch with a small tip will accomplish this nicely. Use Easy solder to preserve the joint that was already made when soldering the half-circles onto the tang.

I made this knife using soft solder for this step. The result has stood up to extreme stress, so I feel confident in saying that soft solder can be used to join the blade to the handle. The trick here is that the tang (with its brass flange) must make a very tight fit into the pipe. The pipe in turn is strengthened by being braced against the guard. If the whole assembly is tight and clean, the soft solder can do a neat and very strong job. Use the appropriate flux and apply heat to the tang, the handle, and the guard all at the same time. You will probably want to have the blade supported vertically in a vise for this operation. Heat only until the solder flows. Allow the blade to cool for about a minute before quenching, then clean off any excess solder.

[9] The knife is finished to suit personal taste. In this case I cleaned the copper with a scouring pad and applied several coats of a heavy-duty spray paint. The brass elements were buffed and the blade was sanded to a #400 grit finish. The 15 feet of nylon cord were bought at a fabric store and wrapped around the handle. A piece of this same cord was tied into the cap and the handle was filled with items that might be handy in a pinch. The selection is dependent on your locale and your personality.

[10] As a final step the blade is honed on a stone. To get proper use from your knife you'll want to make a sheath. See chapter 4 for suggestions on this.

11

PROJECT 6:

Forged Camp Knife

This project introduces the use of the forge and the techniques needed to hot-work steel. The knife is a versatile style and includes a nickel silver guard and butt cap and a leather handle.
This project covers forge use, the making of a flush end nut, and a handle made of stacked leather disks.

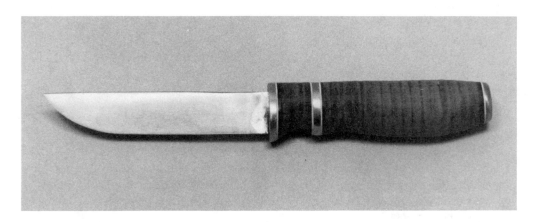

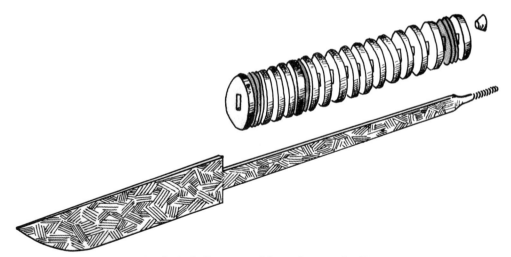

Exploded diagram of forged camp knife.

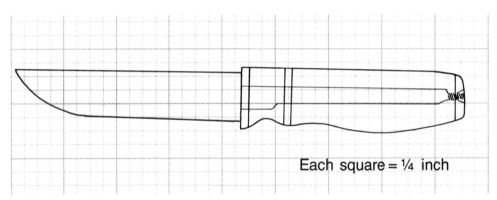

Each square = ¼ inch

Scale drawing of forged camp knife.

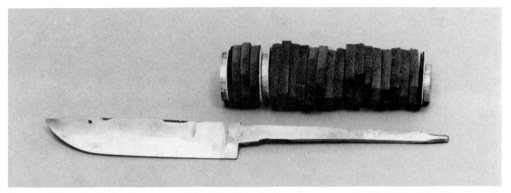

Parts of the knife before assembly. The blade has been rough filed, but further work is needed before heat treating.

LIST OF MATERIALS

Blade: The size of the knife will determine the size of the stock. For this piece I used a piece of coil spring from a truck. Steel in the form of a rod about 2 feet long is easiest to handle.

Guard and butt cap: about 4 square inches of heavy gauge nickel silver or brass sheet

Handle: leather disks, which can be bought precut or made from scrap leather

Fiber spacers: available from a knifemaking supply company.

Principal Tools: forge, anvil, hammer, files, tap and die, jeweler's saw

PROCESS OVERVIEW

1. Build a clean, hot fire in a forge. Draw out the tang.
2. Through careful forging bring the tang to a uniform thickness.
3. Forge the blade.
4. Cut the blade from the stock.
5. Forge the tip of the blade. Normalize.
6. Grind/file the blade bevel. Sand to a medium finish (e.g. #240).
7. Heat-treat the blade. Finish to a finer grit.
8. File/grind the tang to a uniform girth.
9. Saw out the guard(s).
10. Cut out the handle pieces.
11. Cut threads on the end of the tang.
12. Cut threads in the cap nut.
13. File/grind the cap nut to a cone shape.
14. Test-fit all pieces.
15. Assemble the handle, using glue between each layer. Tighten the cap nut.
16. After the glue sets, grind/file the handle to its final shape and finish.
17. Hone the edge.

DESIGN CONSIDERATIONS

The first five projects have been made using the technique called *stock removal,* the grinding away of material to arrive at a given shape. This project and the next represent a totally different approach to knifemaking, called *forging.* In this approach the steel is hammered to shape while it is red-hot. The process involves special tools that are discussed in chapter 5. In addition to a new set of tools, though, forging also calls for a different way of thinking.

With this project we enter the world of the blacksmith, a place of noise, effort, dirt, and exhilaration. Like sauerkraut or oysters, blacksmithing is something you either love or you hate. The process of smithing defies casual interest. The pace, the smells, the feel of the tools in your hands all contribute to a demanding involvement. There's no such thing as a lazy blacksmith. You just can't do it halfway. It requires rigorous involvement and for some people this is what makes it such a special pursuit.

The popular conception of the blacksmith as a burly fellow with bulging biceps should not dissuade anyone from taking up smithing, especially not the making of small items like knives. Good smithing is as much a matter of concentration and skill as brawn. I know many blacksmiths, both men and women, whose size denies the common misconception.

For me a large part of the pleasure of knifesmithing is the radical alteration of a tough material from one shape to another. In the knife shown in this project, for example, the coil spring of a truck has been flattened and thinned so much that it shows no clue of its origin.

This knife is similar in its construction

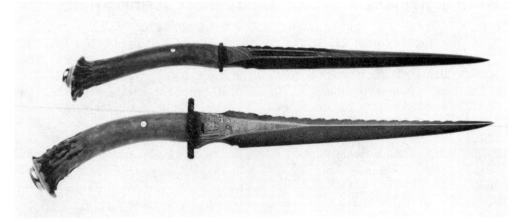

Two stag-handled knives by Scott Lankton. Both use Damascus steel and file work ornamentation, and both have a jade cabochon set in the pommel. (Photo courtesy of the artist)

to Project 4, the Through-Tang Skinner. Both have a skinny tang that extends through the handle and out the back end, where it is capped with a threaded element that holds all the pieces of the handle together. In this project the handle is a lamination of disks of leather. I've also used a double guard arrangement and colored fiber spacers. I have further altered this piece from the earlier example by making a hidden nut for the butt cap.

PROCESS DETAIL

Forging

The forging starts with a more or less straight bar of tool steel about 2 feet long. A car leaf spring will do the trick and of course steel can be bought in this form, ready to go. If you are making your knife from a coil spring, the first step is to unwind the coil. To do this, build a large, hot fire and set the spring in the center of it. When about a 6-inch length of the spring is at a bright red heat, pull it from

the fire and straighten that section. This can be done by hammering over the horn of the anvil, by setting the hot part along or astraddle the anvil, by levering in the hardy hole, or in a two-man approach. Probably some combination of techniques will be needed. When the color has faded, return the steel to the fire and heat another half-foot or so. Because the resulting tangle of metal is large and awkward, fitting it into the forge can present a problem. The best advice I can offer is to be ingenious and work your way through it.

When you have straightened a section about 2 feet long, bring the cutoff point to a bright red. To cut off the piece you will be using, hammer it, at red heat, either on a cutting hardy or against the edge of the anvil. Strike the fulcrum of this arrangement with the flat face of the hammer until a dark line shows through the red of the hot steel. Bend the crease back and forth until the pieces break apart. Allow the stock to cool slowly, at least until it can be handled.

At that point you can quench it and begin the real work of the knife.

[1] Bring the forge to a steady heat. Instruction in this is given in chapter 5. When the fire produces a hot core, slide the tip of the steel bar into the center of the firepot and bring the last 2 to 3 inches to a red orange heat. Turn off the blower and slide the steel out of the fire. Try not to disturb the fire. Moving quickly (but not frantically), set the steel tip on the edge of the anvil, at right angles to it. Strike the steel with an overhanging blow (see drawing). This will begin the necking-in of the tang. The location of the first blow will depend on the length of the intended knife and the mass of the stock with which you've started. It will probably be around 2 to 2½ inches from the end.

The cross-peen of the hammer is used to control the flow of the metal under the hammer blows. The wedge shape of the hammer forces the metal in two directions, as shown in this drawing. Striking blows with the cross-peen at a right angle to the bar will push the metal along its length. This will create a longer, skinnier bar. In the case of a square bar being made into a blade, the cross-peen will be struck parallel to the axis. This has the effect of pushing the metal outward and broadening the rod.

Establish a square section at the neck. Continue this square down the length of the tang, working on all four sides. Do not strike the steel unless it is bright red. Hitting tool steel when it is any cooler risks the creation of internal stresses that can show up later in the finished product. When the color starts to fade, return the bar to the forge and turn on the blower.

This is a real good time to ruin the

A bar of steel can be cut at red heat by setting it over the edge of the anvil like this.

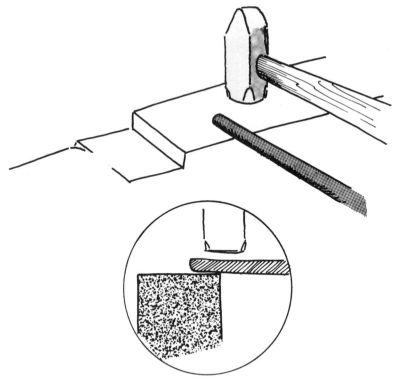

To begin forming the tang, set the end of the steel bar on the anvil and strike an over-hanging blow. This will neck-in or reduce the bar on the underside. By striking similar blows on all sides, a stubby tang is created. Further forging will draw out and shape the tang.

steel. It's so easy any child can do it, and with very little effort you can too! Just leave the steel in the fire for too long and you'll burn it, sure as anything. This can happen very quickly, so you must pay close attention to your work. Until you get the rhythm of the fire, check the steel frequently by sliding it part-way out of the fire. This slows down the heating process and is a habit you will outgrow, but it's better to be cautious at this stage than to waste your steel by burning it. When the steel burns it becomes a spar-kler, throwing off sparks like the Fourth of July. If you strike the steel at this point

it will shatter, sending dangerous pieces in every direction.

If you accidently make a sparkler, bring it out of the fire and allow it to cool for half a minute. Cut off the ruined part and begin again.

Continue forging the tang area, keep-ing it square, until it is the desired length. This takes less time to write about than it does to accomplish. You will probably go back to the fire six or eight times to accomplish this. The tang will be about 6 inches long when you're done and will be roughly a quarter-inch square.

[2] The tang is heated to red and re-

The cross-peen is used to direct the flow of metal under hammer blows, as shown.

duced to a rectangular section with the longer side lying flat with the blade. Use a pair of dividers or the open jaws of a vise as a guide to be sure that the tang is a uniform thickness all along its length. This is an important step if the guard is to make a snug fit. The area where the tang meets the blade usually requires special attention. Excess material here can be filed away later, but reduce the thickness with a hammer as best you can, since it is faster.

[3] Attention is now given to the blade area. The amount of shaping will of

A 14-inch knife of Damascus steel with brass and rosewood by Bob Coogan. (Photo courtesy of the artist)

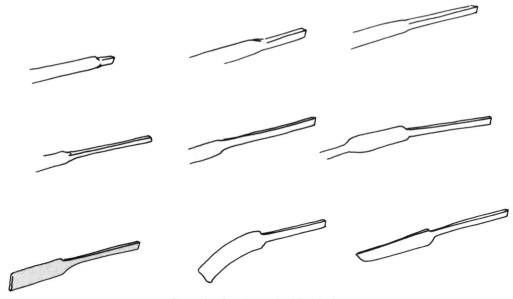

Steps in forging a knife blade.

course depend on the original shape of the steel. If you started with a rectangular bar close in size to your intended blade, very little forging will be needed. If you started with round stock (as I did), the first step will be to forge the rod into a square section. Of course this is done only at red heat. Steel, especially carbon steel, develops a black scale as it is heated. If this scale is allowed to sit on the steel during forging it is pressed into the metal and leaves a roughened surface. To avoid this, the steel is brushed vigorously with a coarse wire brush. This is done as soon as the steel is withdrawn from the fire, before any blows are struck. The scale is thrown off in a shower of sparks, so be sure to direct your brushing away from any bystanders or other combustibles. Because the tang area will be out of sight, it is not as important to wire brush that part.

[4] When the blade shape is roughly established, it is cut off the longer bar. To do this, heat the cutoff area to a bright red and set it either against a cutting fuller or the edge of the anvil.

[5] Your work should begin to look like a knife by now. If it appears that further shaping can be done with hammers you will need tongs to hold the workpiece. Blacksmithing tongs can be bought at flea markets and antique stores or through the suppliers listed at the back of the book. For small occasional work like this, Vise-Grips can also be used.

Heat the knife blank to red and strike it with the hammer to achieve the shape shown in the second to the last drawing in the sequence illustration. The edge that is curved down is then struck. This makes it thinner and causes the curve to straighten out. Further filing of the blade bevel will be required, but this forging will shorten that step.

When the forging is completed the steel is normalized by heating it to a medium red overall. Let it cool slowly. This will allow the grains to assume a more or less uniform size and help to relieve stresses within the steel.

[6] Filing and grinding will be needed to give a final shape to the blade, even when the blacksmith is a master. For beginners it's not unusual to depend heavily on the removal of excess steel to refine the shape. When the silhouette of the knife blank is correct, the bevel of the blade is filed. As usual, pay attention to the ricasso edge and see that the cutting edge of the blade falls at mid-thickness of the steel.

Hardening and Tempering

[7] The blade can be heat-treated in the forge or with a torch as described previously. To use the forge, build up a bright, hot fire. Lift away the top coals of the fire to reveal an exposed mound of glowing coals. Set the blade on top of this and watch as it takes on a red heat. Flip it over once or twice to even out any irregularity of the heat. When the steel is a uniform red orange, quickly pull the blade from the fire and plunge it into a can of oil that has been moved close to the forge. Stir with the steel as before to ensure that fresh, cool oil is constantly brought into contact with the steel.

The tempering process as worked at the forge is a little different. Set a heavy piece of scrap steel into the forge to heat up while you sand the black oxide film off the blade. Allow the large bar to get to at least a dull red heat, brighter in the case of large blades. The bar is pulled from the fire and either laid on the side of the hearth or rested with its tip on the anvil. The knife blade is held with its spine along the bar. When tempering colors first appear, the blade should be turned

A large carving knife by Bob Coogan. The blade is of 440C, the guard is mokume, and the handle is black linen Micarta. (Photo courtesy of the artist)

over to distribute the heat evenly. Allow the tempering colors to spread as described before, manipulating the blade to direct the flow of heat. When the tempering is complete the blade is quenched to halt the action. Before going on to the next step don't forget to move the can of quenching oil away from the forge.

Preparing the Tang

[8] Grind or file the tang to a uniform girth. Use dividers, a sliding gauge, or the open jaws of a vise to register the thickness and width of the tang. It should be exactly the same size all along its length, or it may taper away from the blade. The guard that will sit against the blade will be slid into place along the tang. That's why the tang must be of a consistent thickness and width.

[9] The next step is to saw out the guard. In this case I'm using nickel silver and have made two guards, but many other materials and configurations could be used. The fit of the rectangular hole is critical and deserves care. Mark and saw it out carefully. File until the guard makes a snug fit over the tang and rests squarely against the blade.

[10] Before going any further with the handle, check the tang for length. Cut off any extra. For this knife the handle is made up of oval pieces of leather. I bought scrap belt stock from a leather worker. Other sources would include shoemakers and industrial suppliers where leather belting for machines is sold. Make a cardboard template to give the size of the disk and its rectangular center hole. Trace the shape onto the leather repeatedly with a pen and cut out the disks with a sharp knife. These will be ground to their final shape after

the knife is assembled, so it is not necessary to be precise when cutting the disks. Slide the pieces onto the tang as you work to determine how many disks will be needed.

To add color to this knife I included pieces of a tough fibrous material. This is available through knifemaking suppliers where it is called *spacer material*. Many other materials could be used in this way.

[11] Remove the handle pieces and prepare the end of the tang to receive the fastening nut that will hold the handle together. The last inch of the tang is filed to a cylindrical shape with a chamfer around the top edge. A threading die is used to cut threads on this rod for at least a half-inch section. For a full description of this process, refer to chapter 9.

Making a Flush Nut

[12] It is possible to cap this handle with a commercially made nut as was done in Project 4. In order to present a slightly different approach, I made this knife with a hidden or flush nut made of nickel to blend in with the butt cap. The first step is to purchase a tool used to cut threads on the inside of a hole, called a *tap*. This is sold at hardware stores and should cost under $2. Buy a tap that is the same size, both in diameter and threads per inch, as the die used to thread the end of the tang. While you're at the hardware store, also buy a drill bit matched to the tap. This is important to make a clean, fully threaded hole and to avoid breaking the tap.

Drill the correct size hole in a heavy sheet of nickel silver. This is best done before the nut is cut from the large sheet. The tap is then used to cut threads on the inside of this hole. You can by a T-shaped

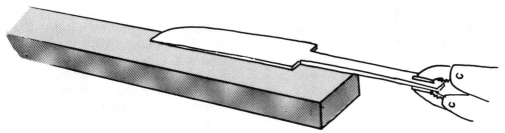

Tempering at the forge is done by setting the blade on a heavy bar of steel that has been heated to red. Work away from the fire itself, since the glow of the coals make it difficult to perceive color.

handle made for holding taps, or you can substitute Vise-Grips for this.

The cutting action is a matter of a half turn forward and a quarter turn back. The unscrewing motion clears away freshly cut chips. Continue cutting, using this screwing-unscrewing action until the tool turns easily.

[13] The nut must be carved to a cone shape to secure the handle pieces tightly. Start by cutting out a circle of metal having the threaded hole as its center. It should be about ¼ inch in diameter. The cone shape can be filed by hand or, as shown in the drawing, by mounting it on a bolt and turning it in a drill. In this

case a file and coarse abrasive papers are used to achieve the shape.

[14] The butt cap is a disk of nickel silver. It was cut from thick sheet with a jeweler's saw. To correspond to the nut that was just made, this piece must have a cone-shaped hole. One way to make this is to use a series of drill bits of decreasing size. Use these carefully so you don't accidently drill through the butt cap. After drilling, a file is used to smooth away the ridges. Another approach uses a jeweler's saw held at an angle to enlarge the hole to a cone shape. Small grinding burrs can be used to smooth and refine the hole. By continually check-

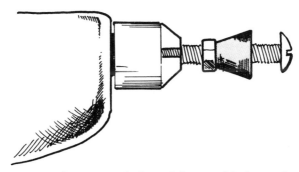

To shape the cone nut, set it up on a bolt and fasten this into a hand drill. By holding a file against the revolving nut, the shape can be quickly achieved.

ing the fit of the cone in its hole you will arrive at a proper fit. The end cap can then be cut from its larger sheet and the pieces of the handle can be given a trial assembly.

Assembling the Handle

[15] If all is in order the handle is taken apart and a generous amount of epoxy is mixed up. Reassemble the handle pieces, this time with a coating of glue between each layer. When the butt cap is set in place, the cone nut is screwed down and tightened. Use pliers to grasp and turn the cone. Allow the glue to set according to the manufacturer's instructions.

[16] The handle is given its intended shape with files or by sanding. Be careful when grinding that the metal parts don't heat up enough to burn the glue. Go slowly, examining the shape for comfort and good looks as you proceed. It's better to create the form slowly than to accidently cut away more material than you intended. When the end of the butt cap is filed and sanded flush, the cone nut will blend in.

[17] The edge should be honed on an oilstone and the knife is finished.

12

PROJECT 7:

Kitchen Chopper

This chapter describes a domestic knife used to chop meat or vegetables. It is a universal form sometimes known by the Eskimo name for such a knife, ooloo. The technique used here differs from the other projects in that the steel of the blade serves as the handle, without the addition of other materials. Another difference is that in this example I have allowed hammer marks to remain on the finished knife. This is not integral to the chopper form but is included to illustrate a possibility for any kind of knife. This project teaches forging, splitting, piercing, twisting, and the carving of steel.

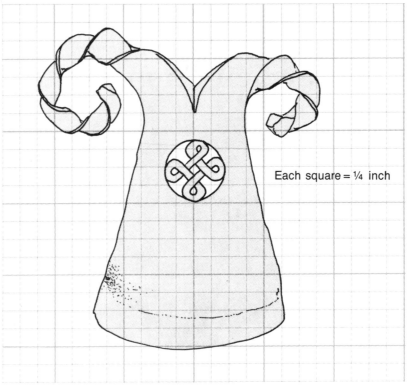

Scale drawing of kitchen chopper.

LIST OF MATERIALS

Blade: piece of tool steel about the size of your hand; ⅛" to ¼" thick. The process is easiest if you work on a long bar that can serve as a handle, cutting off the blade only after the major work is completed.

Principal Tools: forge, Vise-Grips, cross-peen hammer, jeweler's sawframe and blades, small grinding burrs

PROCESS OVERVIEW

1. Build a small, hot fire in the forge. Heat the last 3 to 4 inches of a steel bar, and make a cut down its center for a distance of about 3 inches by striking it against a cutting fuller or the edge of the anvil.
2. Bend the two legs away from each other, bringing one forward to allow access to each leg for forging. Elongate the handle pieces by forging them to a square section and drawing out a taper.
3. At red heat, bend the legs back to their original position and spread them sideways. Reheat and twist each leg. The two twists should turn in opposite directions.
4. Broaden the blade area just below the twist by striking with the cross-peen parallel to the center axis of the bar. Remove large hammer marks to achieve a uniform surface.
5. Cut the workpiece from the bar.
6. Finish forging the blade area, thinning and broadening it.
7. Anneal the steel by heating to red and allowing for a slow cool-down.
8. Clean the chopper with a wire brush. Grind the blade area.

"Bitty Blades #4 & 5" by Michael Croft. These small choppers use 01 steel, brass, Pakawood, and Micarta. (Photo courtesy of the artist)

9. Design and draw the pierced area, lay the design out on the steel, and drill the necessary holes.
10. Pierce.
11. Carve the pattern (optional).
12. Heat-treat.
13. Hone.

DESIGN CONSIDERATIONS

The purpose and uses of this knife are different from those of a paring knife, so of course new factors must be considered in coming up with the design. Usually in a chopping stroke the mass of the knife is more important than the keenness of the edge. A chopper like this can be used on a flat cutting board or with a wooden bowl. In that use it's particularly handy for chopping nuts or dicing vegetables.

One of the reasons for including this project is to illustrate the different approach of using the steel to make its own handle. This kind of self-handled knife is not unique to choppers and is in fact gaining popularity among all shapes of knives.

The piercing demonstrated here is ornamental and could be omitted. By the same token this technique could be used well on just about any other knife in this book. Piercing can stand by itself or can be given greater relief as done here through the use of grinding tools.

PROCESS DETAIL

[1] Because this knife is shaped in the forge, the first step is to build a fire. If you are unfamiliar with this, turn back to chapter 5. You'll need a strong, high heat, so the fire should be allowed to coke up and form a rolling yellow orange bed of coals half-smothered in coke. The steel can be rough-cut from sheet or worked into shape from found material such as a car leaf spring. The example being shown is asymmetrical but you should make your own decisions about the shape you want the knife to take. The possibilities are endless.

Slicing

Forging begins by splitting the bar into the two stalks that will become the

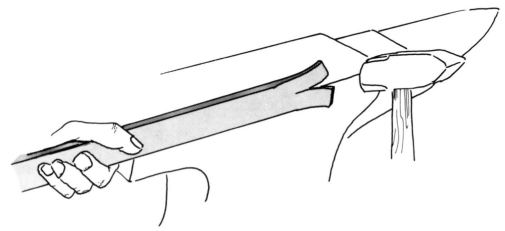

Splitting a bar by striking it against the edge of the anvil.

handle. Remember that carbon steel should not be worked when it has lost its red color. The stresses created by cold working can remain in the steel and cause problems later on.

The cutting is done at red heat with a *cutting fuller* or against the edge of the anvil. Set the red-hot bar on an angle against the edge and strike it with hard, sharp blows. The cut area will show a darker red as it is thinned. It may be possible to cut all the way through in one heat but if the steel cools before the cut

goes through, set it back into the fire and allow it come to red heat again.

Forging

[2] After slicing, the top end of the chopper is again brought to red heat and the arms are pulled outward. Bend one arm forward and the other back as shown. This is done to provide access for the hammer. Working on one side at a time, each leg is forged to a tapering square bar. Depending on the size of

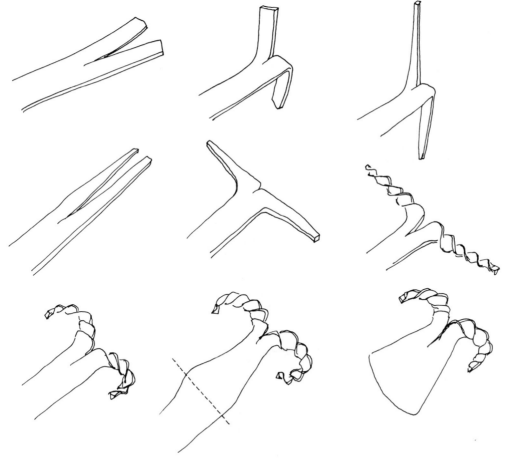

Steps in forging the kitchen chopper.

the fire, the thickness of the steel, and the experience of the smith, this may take as many as ten heats.

Twisting

[3] When the arms have been properly shaped, bend them back to an upright position so that they form a V. At red heat, the blade is quickly pulled from the fire and clamped in a vise. The tip of one of the arms is grabbed with pliers or a wrench and quickly twisted. This process is repeated on the other side, with care being taken to twist in the opposite direction. Remember that there is almost no end to the forming that can be done, but you must work only at red heat. After twisting, the arms are reheated and formed around the horn of the anvil. Vise-Grips can also be used to bend these curls.

[4] To broaden the blade area, the section of the bar below the twist must be heated. It is sometimes possible to slide the workpiece through the fire so that only the area to be worked on is heated. If the shape of the forge doesn't allow for this, another way to achieve the same thing is to lay the steel on top of the fire. Rake the coal around the area to be forged and away from the finished area.

If the twisted arms are red when the bar is pulled from the fire, plunge the twists into a nearby bucket of water for a few seconds to cool them down. If left at red heat they might bend as other sections of the bar are worked.

[5] As described in the previous chapter, the blade is cleaned with a coarse steel brush before any blows are struck. This will create a spray of sparks, so point the brushing away from anything combustible. When the bar is forged to

"Vegetable Chopper" by Lotte Cherin. This high carbon steel utensil illustrates the plastic quality of hot steel. (Photo by Tam Cherin)

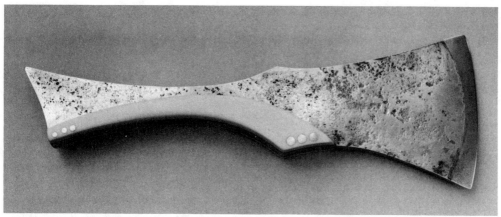

"U-Series, #1 Chopper" by Ken Coleman. This 7½-inch chopper is made of high carbon steel, Micarta, fiber spacers, and nickel silver rivets. (Photo courtesy of the artist)

a shape close to the intended design, bring the steel to a red heat and cut the chopper off the bar. This is done in the same way the vertical slice was made in step 1.

[6] Tongs are now used to hold the chopper by the twisted handles. Heat it to red and forge one more time along the blade. This should finish the thinning and remove any irregularity left from the cutting. When the blade is properly formed, look it over carefully to see that the hammer marks make a consistent pattern.

[7] When the forming is complete and the surface has the intended look, set the chopper back into the fire. Heat it to a uniform medium red to normalize the structure. Cool the blade slowly, ideally by burying it in a bucket of sand or ashes. Allow the steel to cool until it can be comfortably handled. This may take several hours.

[8] When the blade is cool enough to handle in bare hands, the scale can be removed by a brisk rubbing with a coarse wire brush. The lower part of the blade can be filed or ground to a clean sweeping edge.

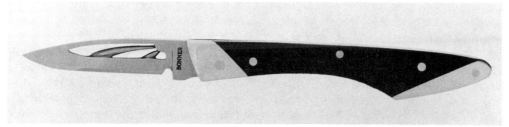

A pocket knife of 01 steel, sterling, and lignum vitae by Jeremy Bonner. Piercing is used not only for decoration, but also to provide a finger grip for opening the blade. (Photo courtesy of the artist)

After piercing the design with the jeweler's saw, it is given relief by careful grinding with a small abrasive wheel.

Piercing

[9] The next step in making the chopper shown here was to pierce a cutout picture in the center of the blade. First I tried out several ideas on paper, keeping in mind that all the parts of the design had to be attached to the sides. The chosen design was copied onto label paper. This was then glued onto the steel and a hole was drilled in each of the compartments.

[10] Use a jeweler's saw with a #4 blade to cut out the design. Lubricate the blade periodically by rubbing it on a piece of wax. This will help it slide through the steel. When the design is pierced it can be refined with a file, but don't rely too heavily on the file to correct sloppy sawing. Your best bet is to control the saw blade in the first place so that little if any filing is needed.

[11] In this example I decided to enhance the relief of the design by carving. A small grinding wheel was used to cut away the steel. The process is not a fast one and hurrying is counter-productive. Allow the tool to shave off tiny bits of steel and the form will slowly emerge. Wear goggles.

Hardening and Tempering

[12] When the design is finished, the whole piece is checked for rough edges and filed as necessary. After smoothing the steel to a coarse sandpaper finish, the blade is ready to be heat-treated either with a torch or in the forge.

Heat the blade to a bright red orange for about 1½ inches from the cutting edge. The chopper is then quenched in either oil or water, depending upon the steel. As soon as the piece can be held in the hands, the black scale is sanded off and the blade is tempered to a plum color. The steel can then be finished with a #320 grit paper.

[13] The final step, as usual, is to hone the chopper on an oilstone. You won't be able to create a razor-sharp edge on a tool as thick as this, but for a chopping blade this is acceptable. This knife will rust if given the chance but if it's dried immediately after being washed, you'll find that it will acquire a deep black patina over the years.

13

PROJECT 8:

A One-Blade Pocket Knife

No one knows exactly when the first folding knife was made, but it's an idea whose time probably came a long time ago. Perhaps more than sheath knives, folders reflect the changing needs of society. One example is the penknife, a small folding knife carried by many people. This was originally used to trim quill pens and was as much a part of office equipment a hundred years ago as a pencil sharpener is today.
This chapter explains the mechanics of a simple folder and describes a see-through mock-up used to test parts before their final assembly. It also covers the technique of etching on brass.

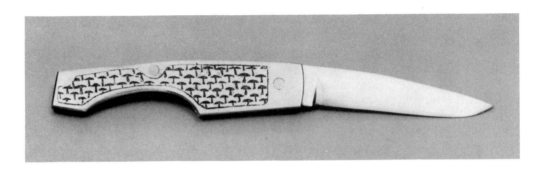

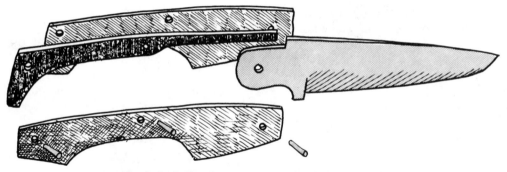

Exploded diagram of one-blade pocket knife.

LIST OF MATERIALS

Blade and spring: a piece of carbon steel about 1/16" x 1" x 3"

Handles: about 6 square inches of thick brass sheet; 14 gauge (about 1/16") is a good size

Templates: enough clear Plexiglas to make both sides of the knife, either 1/8" or 1/4"

Bolts: these will be used to hold the knife pieces together temporarily; they must fit tightly in the holes to be drilled for rivets

Principal Tools: sawframe and blades, drill, files, heat-treating equipment, ferric chloride, permanent marker

PROCESS OVERVIEW

Because of the importance of accuracy, this list of steps is detailed and looks a

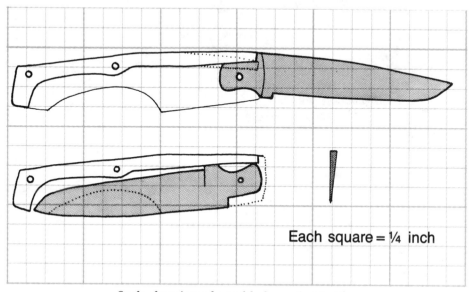

Each square = 1/4 inch

Scale drawing of one-blade pocket knife.

little forbidding. After you've made a few folding knives, however, you'll find the process to be much simpler than this description might imply. Remember to refer to the *Process Detail* for a more complete description of these steps.

1. Design the knife. Use tracing paper to engineer the relationships between the pieces.
2. Check the accuracy of the fit between parts by using tracing paper or acetate. Transfer the outline of the blade and spring onto label paper and stick this onto the steel.
3. Centerpunch and drill holes in the tang and the spring. For this size knife I'd recommend a ¹⁄₁₆-inch hole.
4. With a jeweler's saw, cut out the pieces. File the edges of the steel to refine the shape and remove the cutting marks. Be especially careful in the tang area that the edge is at a right angle to the side.
5. With pliers or a vise, bend the last inch of the spring. Lay the spring on your original drawing to gauge the curve.
6. Harden the spring to a bright red, heating the tip down to at least ¼ inch beyond the first rivet hole.

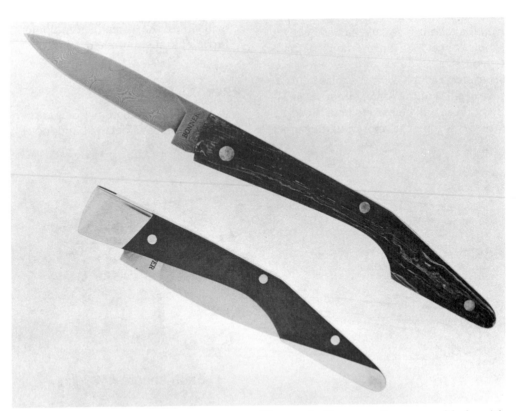

A pair of folding knives by Jeremy Bonner. The top knife uses a Damascus blade with 256 layers. The handle is of deeply etched wrought iron. The bottom knife uses 01 steel, brass, and briar wood. (Photo courtesy of the artist)

Quench in oil. Temper to a bright blue color.

7. Cut 2 rectangles of Plexiglas each slightly larger than the intended knife. Set the spring onto it and mark the location of its two holes. Drill holes through both pieces of Plexiglas to match those in the spring. Do not drill the blade pivot hole yet.

8. Set the spring onto one piece of plastic and fix it there by using bolts. Set the blade against the spring and with a needle or sharp scribe scratch a mark on the plastic where the pivot hole in the tang falls. Remove the blade and make a mark 2 millimeters above the scratch on the plastic. Drill a hole at this point through both pieces of plastic.

9. Reassemble the pieces, this time with the spring sandwiched between the two pieces of Plexiglas. Bolt the assembly together. Fit the blade into the Plexiglas unit. A tapered scribe point is useful in forcing the tang of the blade up against the spring. Test the blade by opening and closing it.

10. When the mechanism of the knife is working, cut/sand the plastic to determine the shape of the knife handle. Refer to your original drawing. Some designs will need a cut-out area to allow for a fingernail grip on the blade.

11. When the plastic handle shape has been fully refined, take the pieces apart. Use the Plexiglas as a template to trace an outline onto the brass pieces that will become the sides of the knife. Carefully mark the location of the holes, then centerpunch and drill them. With a jeweler's saw, cut out the two sides for the knife. Using bolts to hold the pieces together, set the brass in a vise and file the outline to remove the marks left by the saw.

12. If the brass sides are to be decorated as shown in the example, coat all sides and edges of the brass with asphaltum, paint, wax, or permanent marker. Scratch the intended design through this coating, using a needle or scribe. The area that is scratched will be etched into the brass and will appear as a dark line. Be careful to etch the correct sides of the handle slabs.

13. Set the brass into the etchant.

14. Halt the etch and clean the resist off the brass.

15. Attach the spring permanently between the sides of the knife with rivets.

16. Load the blade into the handle and secure it with a rivet. Refer to the text for a method that will prevent the blade rivet from getting so tight it restricts the pivot action.

17. Trim the kick away to allow the blade to retract into the handle.

18. Cut a finger nick into the blade, if needed.

19. Lay a drop of oil into the pivot area and sharpen the blade.

DESIGN CONSIDERATIONS

Variations of folding knives are endless and offer a rich opportunity for design innovation. Before experimenting with any of these delightful variations, it is important to understand the basic mechanism of a folding knife. The accompanying diagrams will illustrate this description.

A folder requires a strip of steel called the *spring* to hold the pieces under ten-

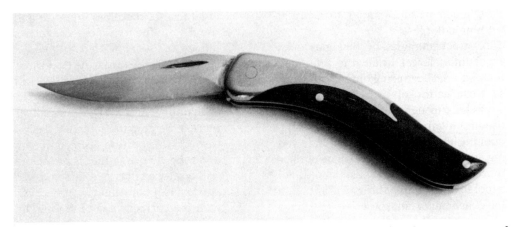

A 5-inch folder by Bob Coogan, of 01 steel, brass, and rosewood. (Photo courtesy of the artist)

sion. This is held in place by one or more *rivets* and pushes down on the blade tang to keep it either firmly closed or firmly open. The lower outline in the drawing shows the position of the spring at rest. The blade is "loaded" into the frame, pressing upward against the spring and creating a tension in the assembled knife. Once assembled, the folding knife is always under tension. If it were not, the blade would wobble around in the handle. The amount of tension in the blade (that is, the amount of pressure needed to open and close the knife) is determined by the tempering, the thickness, and the curve built into the spring. Before any of these factors come into play, however, the effectiveness of the spring depends on the relationship between the tang, the spring, and the location of the pivot hole.

It is important that the pivot lie behind point A as shown so that the pressure of the spring will fall at the point indicated by the arrow. It is because the spring reaches past the pivot to exert its downward pressure that the blade wants to swing up into the handle. The kick area (see illustration) hits against the spring to keep the blade from closing so far that the edge of the blade hits against the spring. Similarly, when the blade is being opened, it is the pressure of the spring against the tang, behind the pivot, that makes the blade want to snap open. This is shown by the shaded arrow (B) in the detail drawing. The shape of the notch in the top of the tang is what keeps the blade from opening too far.

Is the handle shape determined by the blade or is the shape of the blade determined by the handle? Either approach is correct because the two must fit together. The design process can originate in either way. A description of the process of laying out the mechanism begins the *Process Detail* section of this chapter.

The first step, of course, is to come up with a design. As stated above, this can start with a blade shape or with a handle outline. For this example I'll use the outline of an open knife, but keep in mind that because all the pieces must fit together in the end, it doesn't matter whether you design your knife open or closed.

Compactness is usually an important aspect of a folding knife. The reason for making a knife fold in the first place is so it can be tucked away in a pocket or a purse. Folding knives are generally used for a variety of light-duty tasks like opening mail, cutting strings, and peeling apples. Keenness of edge is probably more important than ruggedness. This is a tool to be used in polite society, so good looks are important. Of course there are exceptions to these rules and these should be considered as you design your knife.

PROCESS DETAIL

Laying Out the Mechanism

[1] After sketching some ideas and deciding on your favorite, draw the design to actual size. Make a guess about the location of the pivot hole (refer to the drawing) and use a compass to draw a small circle around this point. The circle should have about a half-inch (12-millimeter) diameter; i.e. a ¼-inch radius. Draw the spring so it lies on the circle at the top and extends beyond the pivot by about ⅛ inch. The tang is drawn, as shown. Note that the back end of the

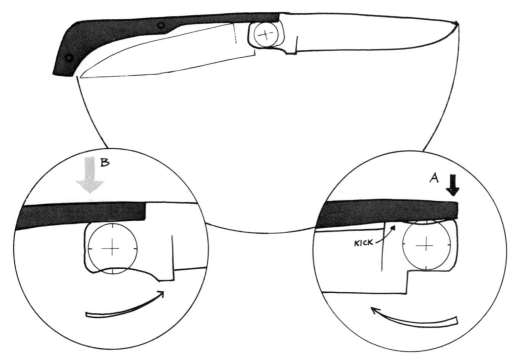

Careful attention to this drawing should explain the workings of a simple folding knife. The arrows at A and B show where the spring is pressing down against the tang. Notice that the end of the spring cannot be in a vertical line with the pivot hole of the blade.

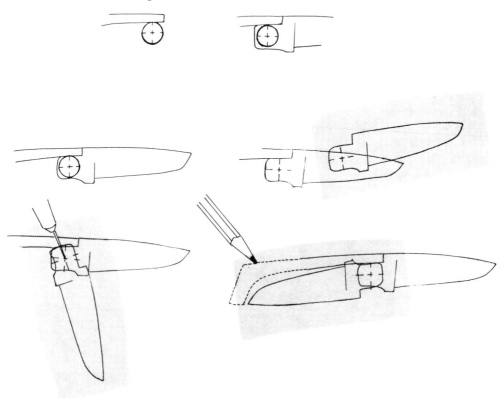

The steps in laying out a folding knife. The shaded area represents tracing paper. Refer to the text for a detailed explanation.

tang is flat and slightly outside the circle. This will allow the blade to stop at a position at a right angle to the handle. This safety measure prevents the blade from closing too quickly. The underside of the tang curves and is adjacent to the area called the kick. Draw this approximation in lightly. It will be clarified in a later step. Determine the size of either the blade or the handle and draw it accurately.

Use tracing paper or drawing acetate to test the interplay of the parts. Acetate is a thin, translucent plastic sold at art supply stores. It is more durable than

paper and makes it easy to transfer a tracing onto label paper.

[2] With a sharp pencil, trace the outline of the blade, including the pivot hole. Set a scribe point at the pivot, and slowly rotate the tracing through the revolution that the blade will follow. As you do this, watch the way the blade moves over the outline of the spring. Refer to the sequence drawings for further explanation.

When the blade has been spun around to its closed position you will be better able to draw the kick and the shape of the handle. This will in turn allow you to define the shape of the nonworking end of the spring. Lift the tracing enough to make a few guidelines on the original drawing, then remove the tracing altogether and complete the blueprint of the knife. Because accuracy is critical here, take the time to repeat this process as often as needed to develop confidence in your layout.

When the design is ready, transfer the outline of the spring and blade onto the steel. The label paper described earlier is especially useful here because it shows a line clearly. Set the tracing upside down onto the label paper and go over the outline with a pencil point. This will leave a faint line on the label. Carbon paper can also be used. Remember to transfer the location of the holes along with the outline shape.

[3] Centerpunch and drill the holes. By doing this right away you will have a large piece of steel to hold onto, which makes drilling a little easier and safer. This also guarantees that the spring will be broad enough around the holes to pro-vide proper strength. Make sure to cut around the holes so at least 1/16 inch of steel remains all around.

[4] Use a saw to cut around the spring and blade shapes, then set each up in a vise and file the edges until they are smooth and line up perfectly with the drawn outline. It is especially important that the tang area be neatly filed. Make certain that the edges here are at a right angle to the flat of the blade. The tip of the spring should make a tight fit into the notch of the tang.

[5] The spring is now bent to create the tension that is so important to the working of a folding knife. I should say here that another way to achieve this same result is to calculate the necessary curve and draw it into the plan, so the spring is cut out in its curved position. This works just as well.

Set the tip of the spring into a vise so the spring projects out to the side. By hand, bend the spring slightly. Remove it from the vise and set it on the original

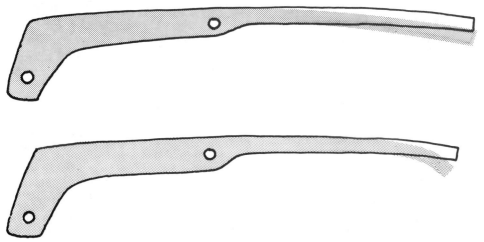

The top example illustrates a proper bend for the spring. In the bottom illustration the bend is too confined.

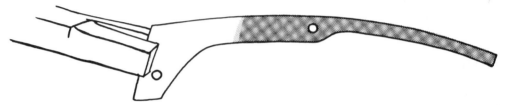

When heat-treating the spring, it is important to harden and temper the area shaded in this drawing. Failure to do so will create stresses around the center hole. This will decrease tension and might even cause the spring to break.

drawing to determine the amount of deformation. You want the tip to be about 2 millimeters (a little less than ⅛ inch) lower than it was before. Pliers can also be used to achieve this. Be careful that the curve is distributed over the whole length of the spring from the mid-hole to the tip. The bottom example in this drawing shows what to avoid. If you bend it too far it is possible to straighten the curve by reversing the direction of the bend.

Heat-Treating the Spring

[6] The spring is hardened by heating it. Grasp it in Vise-Grips at the extreme end of the spring, away from the tip. Be sure to heat the spring from tip to mid-section to an even red orange color. The area around the hole in the middle of the spring is heated as shown. This is important because the area around the hole is frail and if left unhardened will bend as soon as the knife is assembled. This would rob the spring of the tension put into it by its curve. Quench the spring in oil and clean it on a rag or paper towel. Use abrasive paper to remove the black scale that has formed.

Tempering is very important here and must be done with great care. Use a gentle flame so the process does not go too quickly to be controlled. With the spring held as before, play the torch flame over the steel along its length, watching for the first appearance of color. The first shade to show up will be a golden yellow. Move the flame so as to create this color uniformly over the spring, turning it over in your hand to ensure that the flow of heat is evenly spread throughout the steel. The yellow will be followed by brown, then plum, then a bright blue. This is the color you want. If you delay too long, the blue loses its brightness, then turns first dull, then gray. If this happens you'll have to start over with the hardening phase. Careful heat control will allow you to create the blue color just as the torch is taken away. It's like coasting to a stop. If this is not the case, use a water quench to "freeze" the steel at the desired color.

Making a Trial Mock-up

[7] To check the working of the knife without taking a lot of time or wasting valuable materials, use Plexiglas to make a mock-up handle. Besides being cheap and easy to cut, this allows you to see into the knife. This can help in pinpointing trouble spots. Plexiglas is available from plastics dealers or window companies.

Refer to your original drawing and cut out two pieces of plastic, each a little larger than the size of the finished knife handle. Any kind of saw can be used. Set the spring on one sheet of plastic and mark the location of its holes. This can be done with a sharp pencil point if the protective paper is still on the plastic, or it can be scratched on with a needle or scribe. Drill the same size holes as those in the steel. Centerpunching is not necessary. Use this piece as a guide to drill matching holes in the other piece of plastic.

[8] The next step is to assemble the pieces in a temporary handle that will test the working of the knife. The point here is to make the fine adjustments that will give the knife its proper spring. This requires a snug fit. At a hardware store or hobby shop, buy small bolts that exactly match the hole in the knife. Without a stationary spring the mechanism cannot be reliably tested.

To determine the location of the blade pivot hole, set the spring on *top* of the two pieces of plastic and use small bolts to hold it there. Lay the blade firmly against the spring, fitting its notch into the tip of the spring. With a needle, mark the location of the pivot hole. Set the blade aside and mark a spot on the plastic about 2 millimeters above the pivot hole just marked. Be sure to measure from the center of the marked hole to the center of the intended hole. When this has been carefully marked, drill the hole, going through the two pieces of Plexiglas. Take the pieces apart, and remove the paper coating from the plastic if you haven't done so before.

[9] Now it's time to put all the pieces together to see if they work. Set the spring *between* the two pieces of plastic, using the bolts again to clamp them together securely.

To complete the mock-up, the blade is "loaded" into position. The assembly goes a little easier if you use a tapered rod in the blade hole instead of a bolt at this stage of the process. Push the blade into position and slide a scribe point into the pivot hole. Once the tip of the scribe has found its way through to the second piece

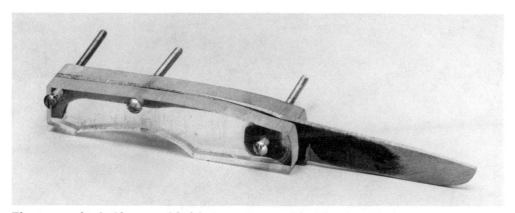

The parts of a knife assembled in a temporary Plexiglas handle. When the action of opening and closing are working properly, the plastic is cut/sanded to the shape of the knife. These pieces can be used as a template for the handle.

of plastic, simply pushing it through will bring the blade up into position.

Test the knife by opening and closing the blade. If the pieces have a burr on their edges, which is common, the feel of the knife will be a little rough. Regardless of this you'll be able to determine if the mechanism is working well enough to be refined. If there are big problems, you'll have to cut out new steel pieces. By looking through the plastic you'll be able to see where a problem lies and whether or not it is repairable on these pieces. Here is what the plastic mock-up should tell us:

If the knife is properly cut out, the blade will snap open and stay firmly there. Some pressure will be needed to close the blade, but it should not require superhuman effort. The flat area at the back of the tang should cause the blade to pause halfway closed. The blade should then snap closed and stay retracted within the handle. At this stage it is good it the kick keeps the blade from closing all the way into the handle. The kick can be filed down as a last step to regulate the depth of the retraction. That is what's supposed to happen.

Assessing Repairs

• If the blade is limp both in its open and closed position, the pivot hole is too

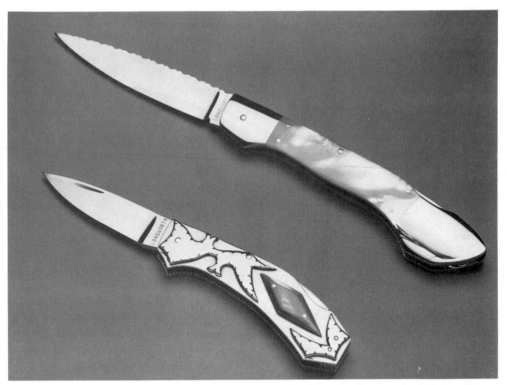

Two folders by Dave Longworth, using 440C, nickel silver, sterling, and abalone. (Photo courtesy of the artist)

far away from the spring. Reposition the spring on the plastic and redrill the pivot. That's an easy one to fix.

• If the tension is too great and the blade is almost impossible to open or close, the pivot hole is too close to the spring. Again, reposition the spring and relocate the pivot hole. Again, that's an easy problem to fix.

• If the spring provides tension for the first opening or two and then goes slack, it probably means you overheated the steel when tempering. Take the assembly apart, bend the spring back into its desired shape (checking against the original plans) and repeat the heat treatment, starting with the hardening. Using the wrong steel for the spring would also cause this problem. It must be a high carbon alloy (about 0.75 to 1%).

• If the blade opens too far and is loose and floppy in its open position, this could be caused by having a space between the tip of the spring and the notch of the tang. If this is the case, the pivot hole is too far forward. Reposition the spring on the plastic and drill a new pivot hole.

• If the blade works in one way but not in another, for instance if it snaps open well but is limp when closed, then you have a problem. The shape of the tang is not correct and needs to be fixed.

In some cases the only alternative is to redraw the blade and cut it out again. It is for this reason that the mock-up is done before spending time sharpening the blade. There are cases, though, where a tang can be repaired, especially if you have experience at silver soldering. Examine your knife and the drawings in this chapter carefully to determine exactly where the problem lies. Don't go any further until you have a good idea of what has to be fixed. If you can't locate the problem now, you probably won't be able to figure it out by looking at the disassembled pieces.

It could be, of course, that you have several problems. If your knife has a couple of the deficiencies listed above, do your best to fix them one at a time. For instance, if the blade never gets enough tension and you also have the problem of an asymmetrical tang, reposition the pivot hole so the smaller area of the tang is properly held. In this case the second half of the solution is to file away part of the tang until the proper tension is achieved in both the open and the closed position. Go about this slowly, testing the blade frequently so you don't remove too much material.

In some cases, the problem cannot be corrected by filing; this is where sol-

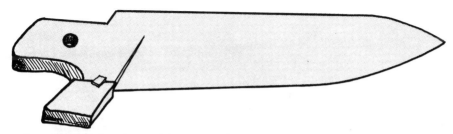

To repair a short kick, silver solder a small piece of steel into position. After soldering and slow cooling it can be cut and filed to shape.

dering skills come in handy. Let's take the common problem of a short kick. If the kick is not long enough to prevent the blade from slamming down onto the spring when the blade snaps closed, the kick must be lengthened. To correct this, cut a small rectangle of steel of the same thickness as the blade. File a flat area on the short kick, and make sure that the little piece to be added also has a flat surface. I use a piece of steel that is large enough to be easily held, even if some of it will have to be cut off later. Coat the joint with a brazing flux (such as Handy Paste Flux) and apply a small piece of silver solder. Hard solder is preferred, but any grade of solder, or even a small piece of brass, can be used. Do not use a soft solder that contains lead or tin. The temperatures of subsequent heat-treatment will cause the solder to come apart.

Use a torch to heat the steel until the solder flows. When the soldering operation has been completed, allow the steel to cool as slowly as possible. This will keep it soft enough to be filed. Set a firebrick on top of the blade or bury it in sand to retard the rate of cooling. When it is cool enough to hold in the hand, cut the kick area roughly to size, file the tang smooth, and set the blade back into the plastic handle.

It is impossible to deal with each of the many problems that can come up in the mechanism of a handmade knife, but perhaps these solutions will provide some help in dealing with whatever problems occur in your work. Keep in mind that the handles are only plastic and that the spring and blade are both expendable. Sometimes starting over is the most efficient way to proceed.

[10] When the knife is working well, cut around the plastic and file it until it is flush with the spring. In a top-quality knife the spring will be flush with the handle in both the open and closed position. Check your knife to see how well you did on this. Adjustments can be made, but for a first knife I wouldn't worry too much about this detail. If the rest of the mechanism is working, leave well enough alone. Cut out the plastic with the blade in or out, depending on the shape of the knife. In some designs the blade is completely enclosed within the handle and in these cases the blade should be set up in the plastic while the excess is being cut away. In other designs the back of the blade is exposed and in this style the blade might be in the way. Either open it or remove it entirely as needed. When the knife sides have been shaped, remove the bolts and take the pieces apart. You can now use the plastic pieces as templates for the handle slabs.

Cutting the Sides

[11] Set a plastic template onto brass sheet and scribe an outline. Mark the holes, then centerpunch and drill them. Cut out the brass pieces, being careful to stay on the line. After cutting, use bolts to hold the two sides in alignment and set the brass in a vise while you file the edges smooth. If you want an undecorated brass handle, skip ahead to the last section, where the assembly process is described. In this example I've added a decorative step that uses acid to etch the brass.

Etching with Ferric Chloride

[12] Typical metal etching uses strong acids to remove selected areas of metal

chemically. A material called a *resist* is used to protect selected areas of the work from being eaten away by the acid. Traditionally the resist is a gooey paint called *asphaltum*. This tarry, slow-drying paint is necessary for strong acids. It will be mentioned again in the next chapter where etching on steel is described.

Here I'll be using a less dangerous chemical called *ferric chloride*, which cuts copper and brass. This is available from an electronic supply company such as Radio Shack. Besides being safer than strong acids, ferric chloride has the advantage of working with mild resists. Any paint, nail polish, wax, and even permanent markers will provide the necessary resist.

In this case I have painted the brass pieces with a permanent marker, giving each side and all the edges a double coat. The acid will find any area you have missed or scratched by accident, so take pains to be thorough. When the ink has dried, scratch through it with a scribe to reveal the metal. This is the area that will be eaten away. Keep in mind that the design will be a reverse of what you are seeing. That is, the bright line against a painted background will be a dark line against the lighter color of the brass in the finished knife.

When the scratching is complete, check the brass again for accidental holes in the paint layer. These are especially likely to occur at the edges. Make repairs as necessary.

[13] Set the brass pieces, design facing down, in a glass or plastic dish (not one you will ever use again for food). Use stones to hold the pieces off the bottom of the dish or suspend it as shown by attaching a loop of wax rod or electrician's tape to the back. Pour the ferric chloride into the dish up to the top edge of the brass. Let the solution work for about half an hour, then check the depth of the etch. To do this, lift the brass out of the acid with tweezers and rinse it off in running water. Set a needle into the

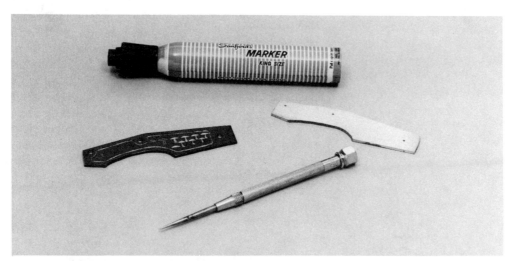

Permanent marker can be used as a resist against ferric chloride. This shows a piece midway in the process.

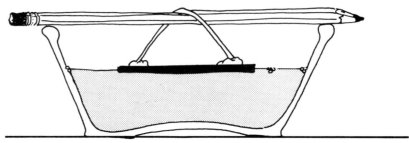

Set the brass face-down in a bath of ferric chloride. A string or wax wire is used to suspend the metal.

etched line to gauge its depth. Allow for later sanding on these pieces by etching extra deep. Return the brass to the dish and continue checking about every fifteen minutes until the proper depth has been achieved.

[14] Rinse the brass in water, then halt the action of the acid by soaking it in ammonia. *Water alone will not stop the acid.* Stir the ammonia around until you are convinced that the whole piece has come into contact with it. The ink can then be removed with turpentine. A torch can also be used to burn off the resist, but beware of inhaling dangerous fumes.

Finish the brass with a fine grit abrasive paper (#600), and if desired give it a high polish by using steel wool or a buffing machine (see chapter 1).

Setting the Rivets

[15] If the rivets that hold the piece together are to be flush with the knife handle, counter-bore a beveled edge around the top of each of the holes in the brass

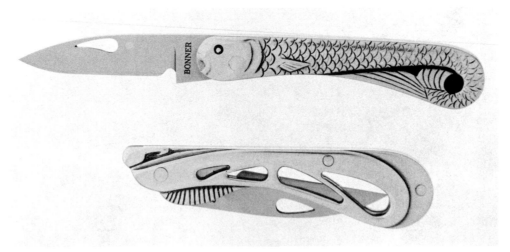

Two folding knives by Jeremy Bonner. The blades are of 01 steel and the handles are of sterling and brass. (Photo courtesy of the artist)

side. As shown in the example, brass rivets may be used to blend into the sides and "disappear." Rivets of a contrasting metal may also be used. Brass, nickel, copper, silver, or steel are all possible.

Set the spring in place and secure it with two rivets, which are made in the same way as explained earlier. The rivet for the blade pivot should be made of steel, brass, or nickel silver. A nail makes a convenient source for a small steel rod. As described in earlier chapters, peen the heads of these rivets over to hold the handle and spring together. Finish by filing and sanding.

[16] Next, press the blade into position and slide the rivet pin into place. By this stage of the process you will have had plenty of practice in doing this. Having a friend help you can make this step easier.

It is the nature of rivets to clamp pieces together. There is a danger of binding the knife sides against the blade so firmly that the pivoting action is seized up. To avoid this make the little spacer tool shown here. This is a scrap of brass that has been hammered as thin as paper. A notch is cut into it, and the tool is slid into the joint so that its two fingers reach on either side of the rivet. Coat it with a drop of oil. The blade rivet is now made as usual, working alternately on both sides. When the rivet head has been well formed, squirt a drop of oil into the joint area and pull the spacer tool out. Work the blade up and down a few times to loosen it and allow the oil to penetrate into the joint.

[17] It might be necessary now to file the kick so the blade will retract all the way into the handle. Go about this slowly, checking frequently so you don't take away more than is needed.

A small wedge of brass is used to prevent the blade rivet from becoming so tight that it restricts the rotation of the blade. Make this by hammering a piece of brass until it is as thin as paper at the tip.

[18] In some designs it is necessary to cut a fingernail grip in the blade. There are many approaches to this. It's possible that the shape of the blade has changed, and an earlier placement could end up being incorrect. Because of this I have purposely left the cutting of the finger nick until the last step. As you become increasingly adept at making folding knives, you may want to cut this grip into the steel before the blade has been hardened. In that case it can be carved with a graver, cut with a saw, or made with a drill. For now we will use a small grinding stone set into a drill. If jewelry equipment is available, use a separating disk. This ⅞-inch wafer of silicon carbide will cut a neat line. Any grinding wheel with a sharp edge can be used. Look in the hardware store for a small wheel mounted on a shaft that fits into a drill. Use a pencil to mark the correct location of the line on the blade and grind a shape that is useful to grasp and pleasing to the eye.

[19] All that remains is for the blade to be sharpened, and you have a knife that you can use with pride. It takes special skill to make a folder and you should be proud of yourself.

14

PROJECT 9:

Lockback Folding Knife

*The locking feature of this knife guards against
a folding blade accidently closing when in use. This
chapter describes the mechanism of this knife. It
also teaches the technique of etching on steel and illustrates Micarta as a handle material.*

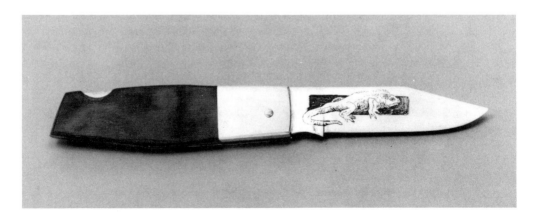

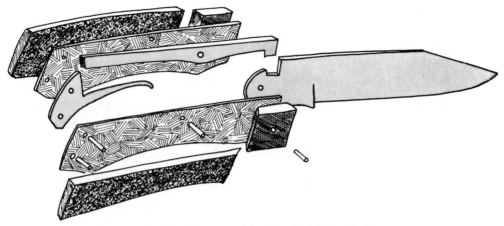

Exploded diagram of lockback folding knife.

LIST OF MATERIALS

Blade: about 4 square inches of any tool steel such as 01, D2, etc. about ⅛" thick

Back: any steel of the same thickness as the blade

Liner: 18 or 20 gauge brass or nickel silver, two pieces the size of the handle

Spring: 01 or similar spring steel

Bolster: heavy (⅛") brass or nickel silver sheet or bar

Handle: two slabs of wood, Micarta, Pakkawood, antler, etc.

Mock handle: two pieces of clear Plexiglas the size of the handle, either ⅛" or ¼"

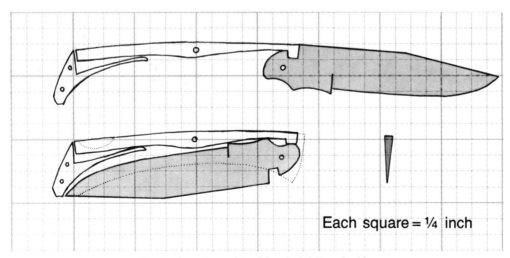

Each square = ¼ inch

Scale drawing of lockback folding knife.

Principal Tools: saw, files, heat-treating equipment, acid, resist, abrasive papers, epoxy, drill bits and matching bolt in ⅛" and 1⁄16"

PROCESS OVERVIEW

1. Design the knife and make a full-size plan.
2. Lay out the design on the steel.
3. Centerpunch and drill the holes, saw out the pieces, and file the edges to a smooth outline.
4. File the spring area to a round cross-section smaller than the thickness of the steel.
5. Harden and temper the whole spring piece.
6. Cut out two pieces of Plexiglas; mark and drill holes for the spring piece and the back.
7. Mark the location of the blade pivot hole, ensuring that the blade is under tension. Set the pieces into the Plexiglas handle and check the operation of the mechanism.
8. After making necessary adjustments, grind the Plexiglas to the shape of the finished handle.
9. Trace the Plexiglas template onto the brass liners and cut them out. Carefully mark, centerpunch, and drill all holes.
10. Cut out the bolsters and file them to shape.
11. Solder the bolsters onto the brass liners.
12. Using the hole in the liner as a guide, drill a hole in each of the bolsters.
13. File the blade bevel.
14. Harden and temper the blade.
15. Coat the blade with asphaltum.
16. Scratch the design through the resist.
17. Etch in aqua regia.
18. Clean off the blade and sand or polish it to the desired finish.
19. Rivet the spring and back into position between the liners.
20. Degrease the liners and glue the slabs into place.
21. Load and rivet the blade in place.
22. Hone.

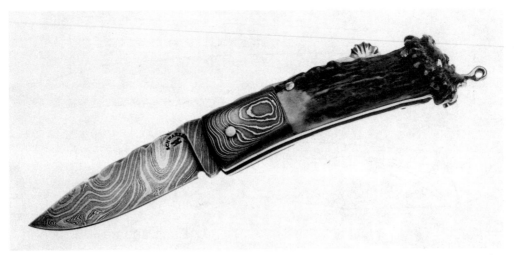

A lockback with Damascus blade and bolster by Stephen C. Schwarzer. (Photo by Weyer of Toledo)

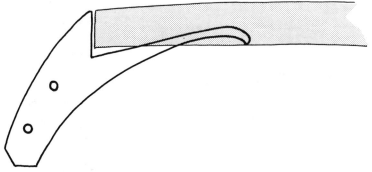

This drawing indicates the position of the spring and back when the mechanism is drawn on paper. When assembled, the back presses down on the spring, supplying the tension that makes the knife work.

DESIGN CONSIDERATIONS

The idea of a folding knife is usually related to small size and portability. Because the handle serves as both hand grip and sheath, the knife is more compact than a fixed blade knife. The drawback of a folding knife is that it is weaker than a fixed blade. The lockback is an attempt to correct this situation by building into the knife a mechanism that makes it impossible for the blade to close accidently. While this knife can never be as rugged as a through-tang fixed blade, it can be made sturdy enough to stand up to heavy use.

Refer to the drawings here to understand the gist of the mechanism. Many variations on this are possible. By experimenting and looking into the workings of a few knives you'll find many opportunities to challenge your knifemaking skills.

As in any folder, the size and shape of the handle is related to the size and shape of the blade. The spring in this example is part of the spacer that sits at the end of the knife. It can also be made as part of the back, or it can be inserted as a piece of spring steel wire (drill rod).

PROCESS DETAIL

[1] The process of designing is similar to that explained in the last chapter. Begin with sketches for the overall shape of the knife, starting either with the blade open or closed. Select a favorite from the initial sketches and draw it to actual size. Use tracing paper or acetate to draw the internal parts. Rotate the blade to see that all the parts fit together. In this case the tension is created by the upward curve of the small, arc-shaped spring toward the back of the handle. It is this springiness that keeps the blade retracted into the handle and makes it snap into its open, locked position. Before the pieces are assembled, or "loaded," this piece should overlap the back of the knife, as shown in the drawing.

Laying Out the Mechanism

[2] When the shapes of the pieces work together, transfer the pattern to the steel.

Remember that your care in layout will be for nothing if you are careless in transferring the design. Use layout dye, label paper, or paper glued onto the steel. The spring piece must be made of either 01 or a similar spring steel. This same material can be used for the back and blade, or another steel can be used. It's important that all the pieces be the same thickness.

[3] Centerpunch and drill the holes. The blade pivot and back pivot should be about ⅛-inch diameter. Because holes this size will not fit onto the small spring piece, a smaller hole is needed there. Remember to plan two holes for the spring to prevent the possibility of rotation. Even a slight movement of this piece would cause a loss of the tension that is needed to secure the blade.

[4] File the spring section so it is slightly thinner than the rest of the piece. This will keep it from rubbing against the insides of the knife. If the spring snags on the liners it won't supply the necessary tension. The arc-shaped spring is filed to a round cross-section. It's important that this is a uniform thickness along its length so the tension is evenly distributed. A thin section would take all the stress and be likely to break. The roundness of the spring will also help prevent warping during heat-treating.

Heat-Treating the Spring

[5] The spring piece is heated to a bright red and quenched in oil. Avoid the temptation of heat-treating only the spring arc. The area where the spring meets the larger section will be under great stress and must not be left brittle. Instead, heat the whole piece to bright red, starting with the larger section, then quench.

Sand off the black scale and temper until the whole piece is a bright blue. Let me emphasize again that the treatment must cover the whole piece. Start again with the larger section and bring that through straw and plum to a bright blue color. Move the torch onto the spring and bring this to a bright blue. This will heat up very quickly, even with a small torch flame. Quench the spring in water or oil to halt the tempering action. A dull blue or blue black indicates that the tempering was hotter or longer than needed. This degree of overtempering will leave the spring mostly annealed and unfit for the knife. If this happens (and it's easy to go too far or too fast), heat the piece to red again and quench in oil, then re-temper.

Making a Trial Mock-Up

[6] Cut two rectangles of Plexiglas large enough to serve as temporary handle pieces. Set the spring and back into position on one piece, mark and drill holes. Lay the blade into position so that it will be under tension when pressed against the back. This can be achieved by making the back piece overlap the spring by about 2 millimeters (¹⁄₁₆ inch). When the Plexiglas is drilled and checked, set it on the other piece of plastic and drill corresponding holes in that.

[7] Set the spring into the handle and bolt it there, as described in the last chapter. Slide the back into place and again secure it with a bolt. Don't tighten this nut so much that it prohibits movement of the back. The blade is then slid up into position, causing the back to pivot down against the spring. This is what puts the blade under tension. Slide a bolt through the blade pivot and loosely

secure it with a nut. Check the operation of the knife to see if all the parts are working. Note that you will have to use a scribe or similar small tool to press down on the back to release the lock. In the final knife there will be a scallop cut along the back of the handle to allow for this.

If there are problems they should show up now. By looking into the handle it is sometimes possible to see what is causing the difficulty. Cautiously analyze the mechanism, checking each component minutely as the blade is rotated through its arc. Think in terms of the relationships between the parts, what does what to what. Don't make any adjustments rashly. Before filing or drilling be sure you understand exactly what the effects of the step will be.

[8] When the mechanism is working, cut/grind the outline of the Plexiglas to the intended shape of the knife handle. Some designs are easiest done with the blade in the open position, while for others it's better to remove the blade. Mark the scallop area that is needed to depress the back when unlocking the blade. This will be cut out when the plastic pieces are disassembled.

[9] Take the mock-up handle apart and cut the release scallop. If there is any question about this, reassemble the mockup. The release should not be any deeper than needed to release the grip, or it will allow the back to show, as illustrated.

Trace the Plexiglas pieces onto the brass liners. Remember to include the location of the holes. Centerpunch and drill the holes, then cut out the brass pieces. Precision is important. Set the two brass pieces together after cutting, align them with bolts, and file the edges until the two pieces match perfectly.

[10] In this example I have used ⅛-inch nickel silver for the bolsters, but heavy brass, stainless steel, or sterling silver could also be used. Trace the brass liners to achieve this shape and cut out two matching pieces. File these to refine their shape. File a bevel on the edge that will fit against the handle slab. This bevel adds an attractive detail to the knife and will help hold the handle slab in place.

[11] Solder the bolsters onto the brass liners, using either silver solder or a soft solder. Whatever you use, be sure you use the correct flux for that solder. The effect of the finished knife will be enhanced or diminished by your care in placing these pieces. It's a sign of good craftsmanship

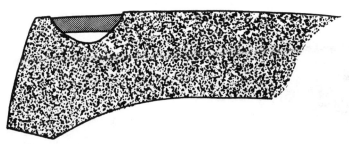

Be careful in cutting out the notch for the lock release. If you go too far you'll create an opening like this.

to have these pieces line up exactly. It is very noticeable if they are even slightly askew.

A strong and good-looking solder joint is the result of clean metal and a good fit. A large amount of solder has very little to do with the strength of a finished joint. In a situation like this, an excess of solder makes a fluid surface on which the pieces slide, so be conservative.

[12] Using the hole in the liners as a guide, drill holes through each of the bolsters. These will be the pivot holes for the blade.

[13] The blade is next filed/ground to its proper bevel. As in all the preceding cases, consider the intended use of the blade to help decide its proper shape. Decide what you want the ricasso section to look like before getting started. After achieving the intended shape, sand it to a #200 grit.

[14] Harden and temper the blade. The tang area should be left soft. One way to manage this is by not heating it to red in the first step of heat-treating. The alternate method is to temper it to a dull blue. Temper the rest of the blade to the range of colors described earlier. Ideally the cutting edge is a deep straw, the area behind that is a plum color and the spine is blue.

Etching the Blade in Aqua Regia

[15] In this example I have decorated the blade with an etched design. If you don't want to do this, skip ahead to step 19.

The process of etching uses acid to attack metal selectively. The acid is called the *mordant* and the substance used to protect areas from the corrosion of the acid is called the *resist* or the *stop*. The action of the acid is called the *bite*.

The last project used acid to etch a pattern onto the brass scales of a knife. In this case it is the steel that is to be etched. The mordant used before, ferric chloride, is not powerful enough to etch steel, so we will be using a very powerful acid called *aqua regia*. I won't even describe the process without first mentioning safety.

Aqua regia is made by mixing three or four parts of *hydrochloric (muriatic)* acid with one part *nitric* acid. The ingredients and the result are Strong Stuff and deserve your most careful attention. Obey these safety rules any time you are mixing or using acid:

• Wear thick rubber gloves and a plastic apron.
• Work in a well-ventilated area, near a water source. A good arrangement is

A skinner with an etched blade by David Boye. The handle is of walnut with inlaid ivory. (Photo courtesy of the artist)

next to a sink in a large room with the windows open.
- Keep a box of baking soda close at hand to neutralize all spills and splashes.
- Store acids in narrow-necked glass containers with thick plastic caps. Always mark the contents boldly and clearly and in several places on the jar. Store the bottles on a low shelf away from direct sunlight.

In the last project, permanent marker was used as the resist. This acid is far too strong for that resist and would eat right through it. Aqua regia requires a more durable material called *asphaltum*. This is a gooey black paint used in paving, roofing, and waterproofing. A source for asphaltum is an art supply store. The resist can also be purchased from most of the jewelry suppliers listed in the back of the book.

Asphaltum is sold as a thick paint, a powder, or a lump called hard ground. The paint is used as it comes, painted onto the surface in a thin layer with a soft brush. The powder is mixed with an equal part melted beeswax to make the lump sold as hard ground. To use this, gently heat the metal to be etched with a flame or on a stove. When the metal is just too hot to hold in your bare hands, the lump is rubbed over the metal. As the wax melts it leaves a trail of resist. Be careful not to overheat the metal, because it will result in a thick layer of wax. You want only a thin film, perhaps $\frac{1}{10}$-millimeter (0.005-inch) thick. Both methods work well and achieve the same result. A disadvantage of the liquid is its slow drying time, which can be several hours to a full day.

[16] The design can be very lightly drawn onto the resist with a soft pencil.

The areas to be etched are then scratched away to reveal bare metal. Bear in mind that the effect at this stage is the opposite of the end result. At this point you see a bright line in contrast to the dark resist. After etching the line will be dark, and the area now covered will be shiny unetched steel.

The point of the scratching is to scrape away the resist. It is not necessary to scratch into the steel. Any pointed tool can be used. A scribe, a biology needle tool, or a sharpened piece of coathanger are all good choices. The size and complexity of your design will determine the right tool for the job.

As you scratch through the resist, be aware of the possible damage being done by the heel of your hand where it rests on the blade. Especially when the resist is applied in a thick waxy layer, it's possible for the tool to plow up a ridge of soft wax on either side of the cut. By accidentally resting your hand on this ridge, it's easy to press it down and fill in the exposed line. Where this is a possibility, lay a piece of paper over the knife to protect it from damage.

When the design has been scratched through the resist, check the blade for scratches and nicks. Don't credit the acid with the ability to know where you want a mark and where you don't. It will attack any spot that is exposed. Pay special attention to the edges. These are hard to cover. Warm the resist in a small container (a can over a light bulb will do) and daub extra resist over any areas that are in question.

[17] A loop of string is used to lay the blade gently into the acid. The exposed surface will immediately become covered with bubbles as the acid starts to work. In some cases this will look like an Alka-

An etched skinner by David Boye. Notice how the images of the handle, the blade, and the sheath relate. (Photo courtesy of the artist)

Seltzer tablet but in others the bubbles are so small they appear as a frosted surface on the steel. Either way you know that the acid is working.

The fumes rising off the acid can do you nothing but harm, so avoid the temptation to hang over the dish and watch the bubbles rise. Allow the acid to work for about fifteen minutes before checking the progress. If you are leaving the room be sure to mark the dish clearly with appropriate warnings.

After about a quarter of an hour, lift the blade out of the acid and flush it well with running water. Hold the blade low in the sink and stand back to avoid any possibility of splashing acid on yourself. After this rinsing, the blade can be held in the hand. Use a needle to probe the depth of the cut. It's probably not very

deep yet but you'll get a sense of the speed of the action. Check to see that all the areas that are supposed to be exposed are being bitten. It's possible to scratch through the wax enough to show a light color but to leave a thin coating of wax on the steel. If this is happening, or if you discover nicks in the resist, correct these now.

Set the blade back in the acid with the string, this time allowing the other side to be facing up. The upward-facing surface usually cuts a little faster than the downward one. For this reason it's good practice to flip the blade periodically. An alternate method is to suspend the blade vertically in the acid vat.

Check the bite again in about a half hour, repeating the process just described. It is a good practice to etch a little deeper than desired in the final product. This will leave room for sanding and buffing of the blade later on.

[18] When the etch is deep enough, rinse the blade carefully in running water. Clean off the resist by dissolving it in kerosene or lacquer thinner. I recommend using the solvent on a small area first to double-check the quality of the bite. If the lines are not etched deeply enough, it's better to have to rework a small area than to make the discovery after wiping the whole drawing away.

The blade is then taken to its final finish through sandpaper and buffing, if desired.

Assembly

[19] Now that the blade is finished, attention can be turned back to the handle pieces. Give the spring a light coating of beeswax or oil to help prevent rusting. Set it into place between the brass liners and rivet the pieces together. In this knife I decided to hide these rivets beneath the handle slabs. I carved a slight counterbore or bevel on each hole. This allows the rivet heads to retain their grip even when filed flat.

Set the steel back of the knife into position and rivet it in the same way. This piece must pivot, so the rivets cannot be set too tightly. Use the forked spacer tool described in the last chapter to prevent the rivet from binding up.

[20] For this knife I used slabs of linen Micarta for the handle. Cut the slabs to a thickness of 3/16 inch and sand them smooth. Use the brass liners to trace the outline of the handle, then cut out the slabs with a jeweler's saw. File the end of the Micarta that lies against the bolsters to a matching angle. This requires periodic checking to be sure the fit is tight. Clean the brass with lacquer thinner and glue the slabs into place with epoxy.

[21] After allowing the full recommended time for the glue to set, finish the handle to a frosted look with files and sandpaper. Set the blade into position and slide a rivet wire into place. Tap the rivet wire with a small hammer to form a head on each end. As before, use a spacer tool during this process to prevent the rivet from binding up the pivoting action of the blade. Sand the rivet heads smooth and lay a drop of oil into the pivot area of the blade and the back.

[22] As a final step the blade is honed.

A lockback folding knife is a complicated animal. Making it successfully from scratch is a demanding task that requires precision and patience. Congratulations!

15

PROJECT 10:

Damascus Steel Dagger

Twenty years ago Damascus steel was a museum curiosity known to relatively few people. Since then an important renaissance has taken place, bringing an appreciation of the material and a knowledge of the techniques to a large audience. Making Damascus steel has in fact become a kind of rite of passage for knifemakers, a proof of skill and dedication. This chapter will briefly outline the history of this steel, then go on to explain how it is made. The resulting blade will be shaped as a dagger and fitted with a fancy sterling mount. As befits the final project in the series, this knife uses almost all the techniques covered in this book.

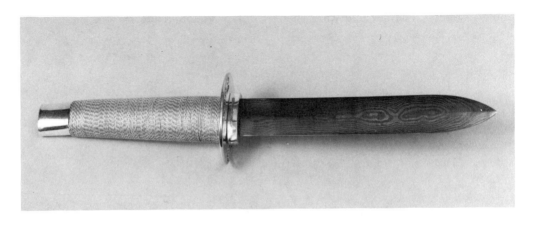

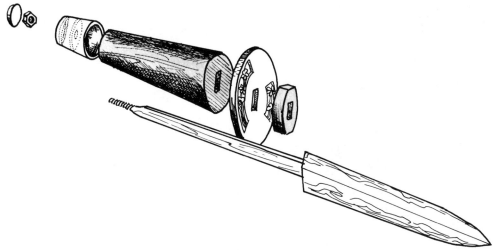

Exploded diagram of Damascus steel dagger.

LIST OF MATERIALS

Blade: two pieces of mild steel, two pieces of 01 or other tool steel; each piece 6″ long, 1″ wide and ³⁄₁₆″ thick

Forging handle: a length of mild steel bar to assist in holding the billet while forging, about 2 feet long and at least ½″ thick

Guard: 3 square inches of 8 gauge (⅛″) sterling silver

Bolster: 1 square inch of 8 gauge sterling sheet

Handle: a block of hardwood about 1″ square and 3″ long

Handle wrapping: 35′ of small-gauge (e.g. 28 B&S) sterling or fine silver wire

Butt cap: about 3 square inches of 20 gauge sterling sheet

Gemstone: a cabochon, in this example an oval 10 x 16 millimeters; any stone and shape may be used

Miscellaneous: epoxy, brass nut, flux

Principal Tools: forge and hammer, files, soldering equipment, sawframe and blades

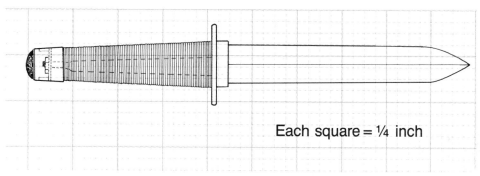

Each square = ¼ inch

Scale drawing of Damascus steel dagger.

A tanto with Damascus blade and bolster by Master Shiva Ki. (Photo courtesy of the artist)

A BRIEF HISTORY

Damascus steel is now coveted for the intricate beauty of its patterns, but the origin of this steel was almost certainly a matter of practical concern. Early methods of refining and alloying steel lacked the high temperatures necessary to reduce iron silicate completely. The result was a coarse-grained material that was unsatisfactory for implements requiring a fine edge and a polished surface. As a common practice, blacksmiths would hammer out material to refine its crystalline structure. Because the hammering thinned the stock, it was necessary to fold the steel over periodically to create enough mass to repeat the pro-

cess. As the steel was continually reheated, it picked up carbon from the fire, creating a high carbon "skin." When it was folded and forge-welded, the "skin" would become a layer or stripe within the steel. After dozens of foldings the steel took on the beautiful patterns we recognize today.

It appears that many cultures independently developed this layered steel, all many centuries ago. Examples have been found in excavations in Scandinavia, Poland, Britain, China, Japan, and around the Mediterranean. The steel was popularized in Europe when it was brought back from the Crusades. It was then linked with the city of its source and acquired the name *Damascus steel*. Because it was widely produced outside that region, the term is unfortunately misleading.

The term is even less appropriate now because the process as popularly done (and described here) does not involve the repeated folding of a single material. In order to create bold and dramatic patterns, it is common now to start with two distinct materials that will make a clear color difference. These are stacked in alternate layers and forge-welded or fused together. Because the point of this process is to create a pattern, the material is properly called *pattern-welded steel*. The word *Damascus* is so entrenched, however, that it is unlikely to be replaced by the technically more accurate term.

In a polished blade of layered steel, the pattern is almost impossible to see. Historically the effects of corrosion, through the atmosphere and handling, wore away the component materials at different rates. This revealed the pattern. It is common practice now to use acid and/or chemical colorants to attack the steel. This hastens the action and gives the knifesmith some control over the look of the finished blade.

The first step is to choose the steels to be used for this project. The difference between the components has a lot to do with the intensity of the pattern. Very unlike materials will create the most obvious distinction between layers. Very unlike materials are also the hardest to fuse together. In selecting steels, the smith seeks a balance between successful joining of the layers and a showy pattern when the blade is finished. Beginners are advised to lean toward the former, ease of welding, for their early attempts. A subtle pattern is better than a blade laced with pits and open seams.

In the example shown I used mild steel and plain carbon tool steel with 1% carbon. These simple steels join fairly easily. Nickel-bearing steels such as ASTMA 203E provide a strong contrast in color but are somewhat tricky to weld.

PROCESS OVERVIEW

1. Prepare the steel pieces.
2. Tack-weld the ends of the stacked steel bars. Weld on a handle.

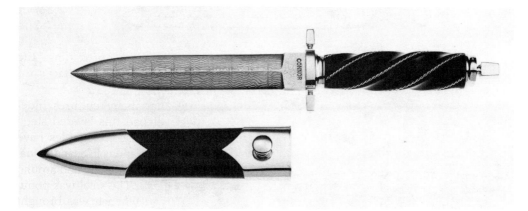

A dagger by Michael Connor. The bolster and fittings on the sheath are of nickel silver, the handle is of wood, and the blade is of Damascus. (Photo courtesy of the artist)

3. Forge-weld the billet. Grind the edges flush.
4. Thin by forging. Cut into two or three pieces.
5. Restack (without folding) and tack-weld the pieces together.
6. Forge-weld.
7. Repeat steps 2 to 6 to achieve the desired lamination. Finish with a bar close to the intended knife size.
8. Normalize and anneal the steel.
9. Cut/grind the blade outline to shape.
10. File/grind the blade bevel. Sand it to a uniform finish.
11. Heat-treat.
12. Finish the blade to a fine grit paper or a buffed finish.
13. Degrease the blade and etch it.
14. File the tang to achieve a uniform thickness and width. Cut threads on the tip of the tang.
15. Cut out the bolster pieces and assemble them with silver solder.
16. Cut out and pierce the guard.
17. Prepare the wood to slide over the tang; file it to shape.
18. Fabricate the butt cap.
19. Twist a length of fine wire.
20. After polishing each component, assemble the handle. Set the stone.
21. Hone and wax the blade.

DESIGN CONSIDERATIONS

Because of the work needed to make pattern-welded steel, it is not used casually. Knifemakers often reserve this precious material for their special pieces and go all out to make a handle and guard that will be as fancy as the steel. There is a potential problem here because the steel, all by itself, is beautiful and com-

Some alternate dagger designs.

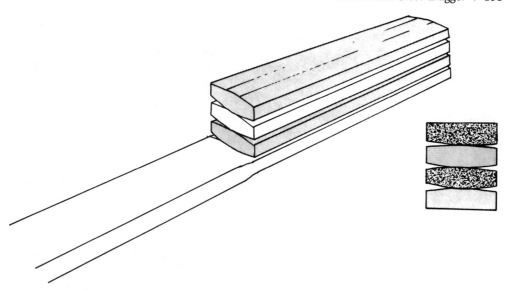

Before stacking the pieces for a billet, grind the surfaces to a rounded crest. This will assist in sloughing off the slag just before fusing.

plicated. A dagger blade makes a good choice for Damascus. Its sleek and simple form does not compete with the wavy pattern of the steel. In this example I've tried to keep my decoration on the guard and handle intricate but secondary to the blade. Of course the degree of success at this, knowing how much you can pack into a design before it becomes overloaded, is a personal decision.

The preceding nine projects are all working knives. They have been and will continue to be used in day-to-day activities. This dagger is an exception. It is a functional knife. It is made of good steel, properly heat-treated and so on. But I wouldn't use it to split kindling any more than I would wear my best clothes to work in the yard. It is like a handmade fabric or an antique lamp. These are things of value that are a pleasure to own and display. The fact that they are functional adds to their interest even though they are not in common use.

PROCESS DETAIL

Preparing the Billet and the Fire

[1] The steel pieces are prepared by grinding a slight bevel or crest, as shown in the drawing. This is done to assist the sloughing off of slag during welding.

[2] The pieces are stacked and tack-welded together with either a gas or electric welding machine. These are the easiest solutions but if they are unavailable the stack may be bolted together as shown. Note that the ends of the stack will not be usable. Plan for this by starting with pieces that are long enough to take this into consideration.

A length of steel bar about 2 feet long is welded onto the stack to act as a handle. It's possible to form this handle by providing a long piece as one of the stacked members. Either way, this handle will make it easier to manipulate the billet while welding and forging. Making Damascus steel involves a good bit of

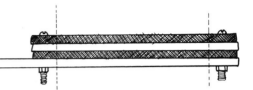

Most laminations are tack-welded together before forge-welding, but it is possible to bolt the pieces together like this. As indicated by the dotted lines, the end sections will not be used in the final piece of Damascus.

shifting of the work in the fire. A fixed handle makes this easier than the usual blacksmithing method of holding work in tongs.

[3] Prepare a clean medium-hot fire. The ideal structure is a "cave fire," an igloo of coke supplied with a generous amount of red orange coals on its floor. Slide the prepared stack into this cave with the laminates vertically oriented. This will allow any slag or ash to fall out of the seams and will help to create a uniform heating.

It is very important that all the pieces in the stack reach welding heat simultaneously. Because the center of the stack will be slower to heat than the outside panels, an even soaking is needed. Watch the stack and flip it over periodically to achieve this uniform heat.

I said before that it's a common mistake to fuss over a fire. The result is usually that more harm than good is done. This is true, but it's also true that good welding requires a broad, even, constant heat. If this is not being achieved, you'll have to make matters right before proceeding. This might be a matter of spreading or reshaping the fire or of adding fuel. Avoid too strong a blast of air. This will cause the outer layers to heat too much and too fast.

Making the Initial Weld

Forge-welding creates a dramatic spray of sparks and hot flux, flying out maybe 15 feet in all directions. Spectators should be warned to stand back. You will want to be completely covered. Wear long sleeves, socks, heavy shoes, and gloves.

It's just plain impossible to explain in words the look of the steel when it's ready to be forge-welded. I've heard welding heat described as a lemon yellow, and to a trained eye that's as good a description as any. The steel will get red, then bright red, then red orange. The next phase is the fluxing heat. It is paler, what you might call yellowish, and hurts the eyes to look at for very long. No matter how much reading you do, the colors of hot steel can be learned only by direct experience. This is not a thing to worry about, but an invitation to get busy at the forge. The sooner you start, the sooner you will become comfortable with the colors you'll see and the meanings they bring to the process.

It's possible to make a few tests to help in determining welding heat. One method is to set a sample of the steel you will be using in the forge. Observe it carefully. When it first starts to give off sparks, it has gone just over the welding temperature. Try this several times until you learn the color and look of the steel just before the sparking occurs.

Another test is to draw the steel from the fire and quickly stab it into the ground. At welding heat, a small shower of sparks will be created. Of course this action takes time and allows the steel to cool, so it is not possible to test and then go right into the weld. Instead it is necessary to reheat the steel to bring it back to the temperature at which the test was successful.

When the stack of laminates has reached a uniform lemon color, pull it from the fire. Lay the bar across the anvil, and give the stack a vigorous brushing with a stiff steel brush. This will send a shower of sparks flying.

Quickly apply a generous amount of borax flux. This is a white powder that can be bought at a chemical supply, jewelry supply company, or sometimes in the supermarket as a laundry additive. Be sure you use pure borax, not a soap with borax added. The borax you buy at the grocery store will probably be hydrated. That is, it contains water chemically bonded in the molecules. When sprinkled onto hot steel, the boiling of the water causes a lot of the flux to be bubbled off.

It is possible to prepare hydrated borax to minimize this. Place a good quantity of borax in a metal can and heat it on top of the forge fire. The water will be driven off, accompanied by a good bit of foaming. When the foaming has stopped, the resulting slag will look like taffy or molasses. After this has cooled, wrap the resulting glasslike chunk in a rag and

Forge-welding is always dramatic. Here Scott Lankton strikes a blow that will help fuse many layers together. (Photo courtesy of the artist)

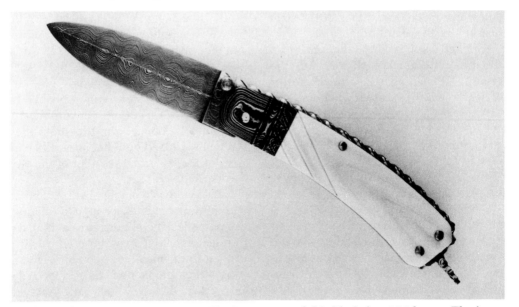

A fighting folder by Barry L. Davis. The Damascus of this blade has 384 layers. The ivory handle and nickel Damascus bolsters are decorated with file work, as are the liners and the spine. (Photo courtesy of the artist)

shatter it with a hammer. Reduce the pieces in this way to a coarse powder. When applied to hot steel, this will stick and flow without bubbling.

It's customary to keep the flux in a can, a bottle, or box near the anvil. Hold the hot steel over the flux container and spoon or pour on a generous amount, allowing the excess to fall back into the box. Flip the stack over and repeat the process. The flux will crackle and bubble as it hits the steel. Return the stack to the fire. The process of brushing and fluxing both sides should take about twenty seconds.

Bring the stack back to welding heat. The stack should again be set in the fire with the layers vertical. If you worked fast when fluxing, not much heat was lost. The reheating should take only a minute or less. Watch closely, because timing is absolutely critical at this stage

of the process. Bring the steel back to the lemon yellow color described above. The flux will be shiny and almost as fluid as water.

Quickly pull the bar from the fire, shaking off excess flux as you swing it over to the anvil. Strike a series of blows in a line down the center of the stack. Follow this with another series of blows along the stack on one side of the center axis. Repeat this in a line on the other side of the center, working your way to the outside edge. Strike as rapidly as possible, using shallow blows.

The power of the blow is not what achieves the union of the layers. Bonding is the result of diffusion at the surfaces of the adjoining parts. The purpose of the blows is to squeeze the parts together. This closes any gaps and allows the crystals of the steels to mingle. Flux aids the action by floating away slag and protecting the steel from oxidation. This is important, since oxygen inhibits diffusion.

When the stack has lost its bright red orange color, brush the billet again and return it to the fire. If the first welding attempt was unsuccessful or only partially successful, it may be possible to repair the stack at this stage. Repeat the process just described, starting by bringing the stack to a lemon yellow color. Add a generous amount of flux. This is needed to clean away the slag that forms with repeated heating.

When the weld is solid, the edges are ground down. This can be done by hot rasping or with a large power machine such as a body grinder. The steel can be worked hot if it is to be held in a vise. Another approach is to slow-cool the billet until it can be handled, then grind it on a bench grinder or sanding machine.

The purpose here is to remove overhanging sections of the layers so they don't get folded over in subsequent welds. Grinding has the added benefit of revealing the quality of the weld. Small gaps, meaning openings too small to slip a fingernail into, will probably close during later welding operations. Larger openings should be rewelded before any thinning is done.

Restacking and Making Further Welds

[4–7] Using conventional blacksmithing techniques and heats, forge the bar to thin it. This will result in a long bar of 4-ply material about an inch wide. Next there are several options. One possibility is to thin the bar and fold it over onto itself. This is not recommended because it will result in a double thickness of a single alloy. This reduces the number of layers and also creates a stripe that is thicker than the rest. This is illustrated in the accompanying drawing.

It's possible to thin the bar to about ⅜ inch, cut it in half and restack those pieces, which will give eight layers. This is illustrated in the drawing. Another possibility is to forge the bar a little more, say to ¼-inch thickness, and cut it into thirds. These three pieces could then be restacked and welded. This would give twelve layers. It is also possible to thin the bar to about ³⁄₁₆ inch and cut it into four pieces. These would be similarly stacked and rewelded. This would give sixteen layers.

The results will look the same, so the choice is one of personal taste. In the case of four pieces restacked, there are few welds to achieve many layers, but each welding operation is complex because

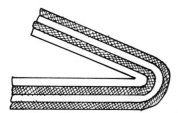
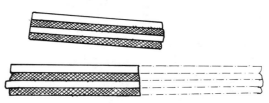

As shown on the left, a folded billet will result in a double layer. Most smiths cut the bar and lay it on top of the first half, as shown at the right.

A small hunter by Stephen C. Schwarzer. The blade and bolster are of Damascus, the handle is stag. (Photo by Weyer of Toledo)

it involves several pieces. The simpler option involves only two pieces, but to get to the same number of layers takes more operations.

In ancient laminated steels the number of layers directly affected the quality of the steel. A fine-grained material was stronger than a coarse-grained one. More layers meant a better steel. The purpose here is entirely visual, so the question of how many layers to create takes on a different cast.

A Damascus pattern of over four hundred layers becomes so subtle it is difficult to see. The skill required is great and the effect is worthy but, like a fine wine, an educated taste is needed to appreciate it fully. Steels with fewer than eight layers create an image that is so large it looks more like a camouflage pattern than a refinement of the material. That leaves plenty of working room. Because the steel is being doubled or tripled with each welding, the layer count increases rapidly. In this example I started with 4 layers, doubled it to 8, then doub-

led this again to 16. If I'd kept going, doubling each time, the count would have gone 32, 64, 128, 256, and 512. That last figure would have required eight welding operations.

In the project dagger shown I made a stack of sixteen layers, then filed the blade shape from it. Pure and simple. It is also possible to manipulate the layers in many ways to develop patterns that are simply dazzling, as shown in some of these photographs. Pattern development involves twisting and rewelding elements, selective grinding and piercing, and unusual folding. These variations are beyond the scope of this book, but several of the volumes and periodicals listed in the bibliography will provide details for interested knifesmiths.

[8] When the intended number of layers has been achieved, the bar is given a final forging to straighten it. It is then brought to a uniform red glow and held at that temperature for about five minutes. This heat-soaking will normalize the crystals, allowing them to find a common size and

orientation. The steel is then reheated to a medium red and immediately buried in a bucket of ashes to anneal it. Slow cooling will relieve any remaining stresses and leave the stock ready for cold working.

Shaping Blade and Tang

[9] Draw the shape of the blade on the steel with chalk or a soapstone pencil and cut it out. Do not use the steel at either end of the billet, where the initial welds that tacked the pieces together were made. This steel is not only lacking in pattern, but it is also coarse and brittle. In this case I used the Damascus for the whole tang as shown in the exploded drawing at the beginning of the chapter. It is not uncommon to reserve the patterned material for the areas that will show and to weld on a piece of tool steel for the tang. The design of your knife, your skills as a blacksmith, and the tools available to you will all determine how you go about shaping the blade.

[10] File/grind the blade bevel. The shape is given first attention, as in all the preceding projects. Refine the surface through a sequence of progressively finer abrasives, ending with something in the 200s.

Hardening and Tempering

[11] Heat-treat the blade in the usual manner for plain carbon tool steel. Refer to one of the earlier projects for a full description. In theory it should be possible to temper this blade to a harder-than-usual color, say, straw color instead of plum. This is because the mild steel that makes up half the blade does not harden and therefore will provide flexible backup for the otherwise brittle tool steel. In practice it's likely that the mild steel picked up some carbon from the fire, making it somewhat brittle. Because I'm not after the ultimate shaving instrument here, I'll hedge my bets by tempering in the usual manner, looking for a brownish plum color on the cutting edges, with a blue color along the spine.

[12] After heat-treating, finish the blade with abrasive papers and, if desired, with a buffing machine. In this case I hand-sanded to #400 grit, then machine-buffed with an emery compound.

Etching to Reveal Pattern

[13] The next step is to reveal the pattern by etching. This works in two ways. Acids will attack and darken one kind of steel faster than another. The surface is flush but two-toned. Acid will also

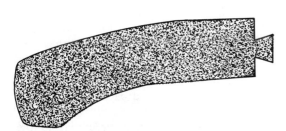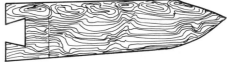

Some knifemakers splice simple tool steel onto Damascus blades in order to conserve material. A straight weld will work, but a dovetail join like this is especially stable.

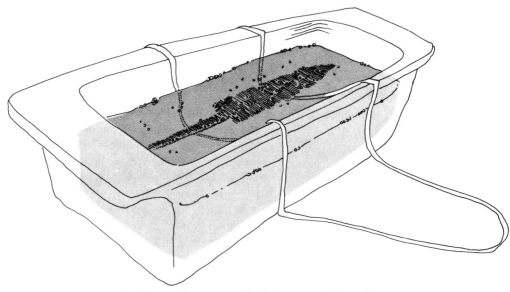

Etching a Damascus blade to reveal its pattern.

attack and remove one steel faster than another, making it possible to create a topographic or relief pattern. This usually includes a color difference but shows the pattern more dramatically because of the tiny shadows created between layers. The effect depends partly on the material used and partly on the duration of the etching.

Proper etching requires that the surface be free of oils, including those left from handling. Degrease the blade with an alcohol-based solvent, then avoid touching the steel. Finger oils, even though they can't be seen, can cause an irregular etch.

A popular solution for etching uses 1 part (15%) nitric acid, 1 part (15%) hydrochloric acid, and 5 parts (70%) water. The solution is used warm. Dip the blade into the acid and watch for bubbles. There should be some bubbling, like a soft drink, but not a violent corrosion. If the bubbles are so thick they obscure the piece, remove the blade and either dilute the acid or let it cool down, or both.

Remember, acids are dangerous substances. The rules for their safe use cannot be repeated too often.

- Always add acid to water, not the reverse.
- Never stand directly over acid. Avoid breathing the fumes.
- Active ventilation and respirators are recommended.
- Wear rubber gloves.
- Work near a source of water so you can immediately flush spills.
- Keep baking soda handy to neutralize spills.
- Always label acid carefully and store it in a safe place.
- To dispose of acid, return it to the manufacturer or supplier, or consult your local fire department.

After fifteen or twenty minutes, remove the blade from the acid bath. Allow excess acid to drip back into the bath, then immediately flush the steel with running water. During etching the blade develops a layer of gray sludge. This can be wiped off on a paper towel, and the pattern will be pretty obvious. If it is still vague, return the piece to the acid for another five or ten minutes.

If the etching is topographic, that is, if some layers are lower than others, the blade can be polished with fine abrasive paper or a stiff buffing wheel. This will reach and polish the raised areas without touching the lower ones. If the pattern is revealed only because of color difference, don't buff or resand. You will remove the result of the etching.

Some knifemakers use chemical solutions to color their steel. The best and easiest to obtain is gun coloring, which can be bought from a sporting goods store. It is available in several colors. The most common are blue and plum brown. These solutions will affect different steels in different ways, so experimentation will be needed to determine the temperature and duration of exposure that works best for you. A typical approach is to apply the solution at room temperature as it comes from the bottle. Allow it to work for about ten minutes, then wipe it off. If the result is not dark enough, try a longer period of exposure to the chemical. If the effect is too dark, dilute the solution with water or shorten the exposure time, or both.

Before going on to subsequent steps, it's a good idea to protect the blade from damage by wrapping it in leather or cardboard held on with tape. Don't stick the tape directly to the blade since the adhesive can discolor the finish.

Bolster and Guard

[14] Use a calipers or similar gauge to ensure that the tang has a consistent width and thickness. This is necessary if the bolster and guard are to make a tight fit at the base of the blade. Any irregularities in the tang must be filed out. As shown in Projects 4 and 6, the end of the tang is filed round and threaded.

[15] In this example I have included a short bolster. Make this from several pieces of thick sterling silver. Assemble it with silver solder and file it to shape. Finish the bolster to a #500 grit sandpaper and, if desired, buff it.

[16] The oval-shaped guard is now designed and drawn onto label paper. Stick this to a sheet of thick sterling and cut it out. Drill a hole in each of the compartments of the design, and cut out each area with a jeweler's saw. Cut the center rectangle with care and file it until the piece slides snugly onto the tang.

Assembling the Handle

[17] Make the handle by wrapping a twist of fine wire over a wooden base. The wood will not show so it should be selected on the basis of strength. Here I used maple. There are at least two ways to make the slot that runs down the center of the handle, and both are described elsewhere in this book. One is shown in the third project. In this case the wood was split and a shallow groove was carved into each half. The halves were then glued together with the grooves in alignment.

The alternate approach is that used in the fourth project. A pair of holes are drilled, one above the other, through the wooden block. The bridge of wood between the holes is cut away with a modified rasp to create an oval slot. For this dagger either method will work.

When the block slides onto the tang it is ready to be given its final shape. This is done with power sanders, rasps, files, and eventually sandpaper. The wood is then sealed with several coats of linseed oil.

[18] Fabricate the butt cap from pieces of sterling silver. This repeats the techniques illustrated for making a ferrule in the third project. Wrap heavy paper around the wooden handle to make a pattern. Trace this onto the sterling sheet and cut it out with a jeweler's saw. Bend the sheet around and solder it into a closed tube. Bend it to the correct shape and check it against the wooden handle for fit.

Cut an oval from brass sheet in a size that will drop about halfway into the cap. Solder this in place. It becomes the surface against which the nut that holds the handle together will tighten. Of course sterling could be used for this piece, but because it will not be seen, brass was substituted. Check the fit again and drill a hole in the brass.

In order to lift the stone above the nut, lay a loop of wire inside the cap. This makes a bearing for the stone to rest upon. Clean the cap with fine abrasive papers and polish it according to conventional jewelrymaking techniques.

If all this sounds oversimplified, you're right. The techniques just outlined would take half a book to describe fully. Space does not permit a full elaboration here. I refer those readers unfamiliar with jewelrymaking to the books listed in the bibliography. Consult with a metalsmith, or find instruction in these skills and learn how to do them correctly. In the meantime you could get by with a cap made of a single sheet of thick material. Borrow ideas from preceding projects and adapt them with your personal innovations.

[19] For the handle of this dagger, I used 28 gauge fine silver wire. To determine the length needed, wrap the handle with a copper wire of about the same diameter as the twist you plan to use. Measure this and add a few feet for insurance. The twisting is done by tightening the two ends of a length of wire into

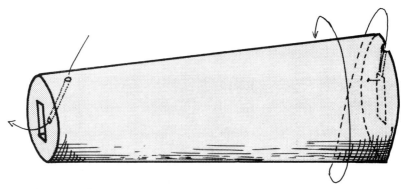

The twisted wire is fitted into the wooden core of the handle.

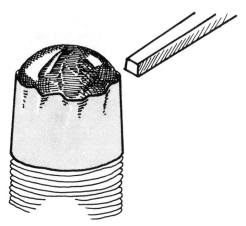

A cabochon stone midway in the setting process.

a vise. Find the midpoint of the resulting loop and clamp this into an electric drill. Run the drill at a low speed while keeping a slight backward tension on the wire.

[20] Trial-fit the components again, then give all parts a final polish. Start the assembly with the bolster, followed by the guard. Slip the wooden handle on in such a way that one end of the twisted wire fits into the rectangular slot. Use a small nick in the wood to allow the twist to make a clean fit against the guard. Wrap the wire neatly around the wooden shaft, keeping it pulled tight as you go. Hold the wire at the other end by passing it through a small hole drilled into the wood at such an angle that the wire emerges out the end, as shown. Pull the wire up tight and bend sharply to anchor it in place. It is trapped under the butt cap, which is set on with the threaded tip of the tang poking through its center hole. Tighten a brass nut onto the tang. This secures the handle assembly.

Lay the stone into position. The cap may have been pushed in during the assembling of the handle. If the stone doesn't fit into the cap easily, use a blunt tool to reach into the cap and "roll" the edges outward. If the stone still doesn't fit in, it may be necessary to enlarge the opening with a small burr or abrasive wheel.

The stone is set by pressing the rim of metal (called a bezel) over onto it. This is done with a simple tool called a *bezel pusher*. This is a blunt length of unhardened square steel rod set into a bulbous handle. The illustration shows the setting midway in the process. Again, this is a dangerously quick description of a complicated technique. The reader is advised to seek further explanation from a jewelry text.

Remove marks accidently made in this last operation with polishing equipment. Silicon carbide abrasive papers will scratch virtually all gemstones. Don't use them near a stone, no matter how much control you think you have. Remove marks with a buffing machine or a small wheel made of pumice suspended in a rubber compound.

[21] The edge is honed in the usual manner and the blade is protected from further color change with a light coat of wax. I use Butcher's Wax, a commercial preparation intended for wood furniture, or a mix of equal parts of beeswax and turpentine. The wax is applied, allowed to dry for a minute, then rubbed off.

Well, that's it; a guided tour through some of the techniques of knifemaking. We've been through the kitchen, out in the backyard, and deep into the woods.

Along the way I suspect you've gotten dirty, probably cut yourself once or twice, and encountered some interesting bits of history.

Knifemaking, as a hobby or a profession, exists for everyone. I hope this book opens a new door to this invigorating pursuit. By learning from others and sharing what you've learned, your enthusiasm will be sustained and your enjoyment heightened. Whatever involvement you find in knifemaking, I hope it brings you many years of satisfaction.

Glossary

anneal – to render a metal malleable by heating. At a temperature that is about ⅔ of its melting point, most metals will recrystallize to create an orderly and workable structure. In the case of steel, annealing temperature is about 50°F above the temperature of final ferrite stability.

aqua regia ("royal water") – a very strong acid used to etch steel. It is made by mixing 4 parts of hydrochloric acid with 1 part nitric acid. See chapter 14 for a fuller explanation and safety rules.

Arkansas stone – a natural, very hard stone used to sharpen steel. The mineralogical name is *novaculite* but it is commonly known by the state of its origin.

asphaltum – a black resin used to mask areas when etching. It is available as a gooey paint or, mixed with wax, as a lump called hard ground.

austenite – a solid solution of steel in which small carbon atoms are trapped within larger iron atoms. This structure is generally unstable at room temperature. It is a phase through which steel passes on the way to becoming hard martensite or soft pearlite or ferrite.

bezel – the rim of metal that surrounds and secures a gemstone.

bite – the action of an acid when etching.

bolster – a plate of metal used to reinforce a knife where the blade meets the handle.

Bowie knife – a particular style of knife made famous by the legend of the frontiersman, Jim Bowie. The knife is characterized by a long, broad blade and a squarish handle.

brass – an alloy of copper and zinc. Alloys with above 30% zinc are tough and are generally machined. Alloys with less than 30% zinc have a more golden color and are preferred for handcrafting. Some popular alloys are called cartridge brass, Nu-Gold, and red brass.

buff – to polish to a highly reflective shine.

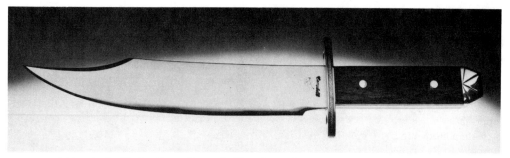

A Bowie knife by Don Campbell. (Photo by Gene Fletcher Brownell)

Though this can be done by hand, it is commonly thought of as a machine process.

buffing stick – a polishing tool made by gluing a strip of leather onto a thin board about the size of a ruler. The leather is impregnated with a buffing compound such as tripoli.

butt, butt cap – the fixture, generally metal, at the end of the tang of a knife. Its purpose is to balance the weight of the blade and to contribute to the design of a knife. In some cases it is considered a functional part of the knife, used for pounding.

"C" scale – this refers to the dial of a Rockwell testing machine on which is indicated the degree of penetration of a diamond point under a specific load.

casing – a leatherworking process in which moisture is allowed to penetrate the pores of the material. This is done before molding.

cast iron – an alloy containing between 2% and 4½% carbon. It is hard and brittle.

chamfer – to remove an edge or corner; to bevel.

choil – a curved edge on the ricasso of a knife that allows a comfortable finger grip.

clinkers – the unburnable residue of blacksmith's coal. It is pale, lightweight, and porous.

coke – the combustible material that remains when volatile matter has been burned out of blacksmith's coal. It is black and lightweight and tends to fuse into lumps.

corrosion resistance – the ability of a steel to resist the formation of oxides. Steels with high corrosion resistance are commonly called "stainless."

critical temperature – the point at which carbide particles in steel begin to dissolve into their surrounding matrix, creating the phase called *austenite*. The temperature range in which this austenizing takes place is called the *critical range*.

cutlers' rivet – a fastening device that consists of two nail-shaped parts. A solid shaft on one part makes a press fit into a hollow shaft on the other part. They are commonly available in brass and nickel silver.

Damacus – the name given to *pattern-welded steel*, a laminated structure known for its intricate patterns.

decalescence point – in heat-treating steel, the temperature at which pearlite changes into austenite.

ferric chloride – a corrosive substance used to etch copper and brass. It can be purchased as a ready-to-use liquid or as lumps that must be dissolved in water.

ferrite – a relatively soft solid solution in which carbon atoms are trapped between body-centered cubic iron crystals.

file work – decorative patterns created by selective removal of small areas of steel with a file. In knifemaking this usually refers to small-scale ornamentation on edges.

flux – a chemical intended to prevent the formation of oxides as a metal is heated.

There are many fluxes, each designed to operate within a specific temperature range and in conjunction with a specific solder.

forge – to shape metal while it is red-hot. This term also refers to the hearth on which a fire is maintained for the purpose of heating metal.

fuller – a steel tool used by a blacksmith to create a groove in hot metal. The resulting groove is also called a fuller. In fact there are many kinds of fullers, including forming and cutting fullers.

full-tang – a style of knife construction in which the steel of the blade extends through the full shape of the handle. This is generally recognized as the strongest of all blade configurations.

grains – in metallurgy, a cluster of crystals with a common orientation. Grain size is important to knifemakers because grain size affects the strength of a metal. A large-grain structure, because it has fewer grain boundaries, is not as strong as a small-grained material.

guard – a cross-piece that separates the handle from the blade of a knife or sword and protects the user's hand. In swords this is also called the hilt.

harden – to cause a change in the crystal structure of steel that increases its wear resistance and toughness. This is commonly done through quenching the steel when it has reached a specific temperature, the critical temperature.

hard ground – a solid mixture of asphaltum and wax. It is rubbed onto a warmed piece of metal to create a layer of resist. This is decorated by scratching some areas of the resist away, and the piece is exposed to acid.

hardness – the ability of a material to resist penetration.

heat sink – a material used to absorb or draw heat away. In tempering, for instance, a scrap of steel could be laid across a thin section of a blade to protect it from overheating.

heat soaking – a practice of holding a metal at an elevated temperature for a prolonged time. This is done for any of several reasons. In tool steel the purpose is often to alter grain size.

hollow ground – a concave cross-sectional shape on a blade. This popular shape offers a thin and therefore potentially very sharp edge. It is made on a grinding wheel or sanding belt.

India stone – a whetstone of synthetic materials, commonly called an oilstone.

latigo – a kind of vegetable-tanned, undyed leather.

lay out – to arrange or draw the pieces. There is an important distinction between this and designing. Designing is a conceptual activity. Once it has been done, the pieces of the design can be *laid out.*

layout dye – an alcohol-based paint used to facilitate marking on metal. This paint, often blue, is brushed onto steel where it quickly dries. A sharp point like a scribe will leave a bright, highly visible line when scratched through this.

martensite – a phase of hardened metal. In the case of steel it is formed by quenching the material when it is heated to the critical range. The result is a tough, brittle material that, when viewed under a microscope, resembles a pile of straw.

Micarta – a trade name for a durable plastic material popularly used for knife handles.

Moh's Scale – a system of relative hardness between substances. This scale was devised for mineral identification and uses ten minerals to demarcate points on a continuum that runs from talc (#1) to diamond (#10). Annealed steel is about 5 on the scale, hardened steel is about 8, and tempered steel is about 6½.

needle files – small files between 4 and 6 inches long. They are available in many shapes and several degrees of coarseness. Needle files are measured by their whole length, but other files are measured by the toothed section.

nickel silver—also called German silver or white brass, this is a popular bolster and butt cap material. It is an alloy of copper, zinc, and nickel (no silver). It is corrosion-resistant, tough, and relatively inexpensive.

normalizing—the process used to relieve stresses in steel. The material is heated to about 100 degrees above its critical temperature and allowed to cool in air. This creates an even grain pattern and a malleable steel.

oilstone—the general term for hard stones, both synthetic and natural, used to sharpen blades. They are soaked with oil to help float away particles of steel.

Pakkawood—a trade name for a handle material made of wood impregnated with plastic resin.

partial-tang—a style of knife construction in which the tang extends partway into the handle. The tang can be a narrow shaft that is enclosed in the handle or as wide as the handle.

pearlite—the relatively soft phase of annealed steel made up of ferrite and cementite.

pickling—the cleaning of a metal with a dilute acid. Its purpose is usually to remove oxides formed during heating.

plain carbon steel—a simple steel in which the major alloying ingredient is between 0.5 and 1.5% carbon.

pommel—a large butt cap.

precision-ground flat stock—the commercial designation for a high-quality grade of simple tool steel. It is generally available in 01 (oil-hardening) and A2 (air-hardening).

quillon—that portion of a guard that extends out from the handle of a knife or sword. Knives can have single or double quillons.

resist—the acidproof material used to protect metal when etching. For strong acids a common resist is asphaltum. For a weaker substance like ferric chloride, paint, contact paper, nail polish, and permanent marker can be used as resists.

ricasso—the section of unsharpened blade adjacent to the handle of a knife. Its purpose is to strengthen the blade. It also facilitates sharpening since that section of the blade, if sharpened, is difficult to reach when whetting.

rivet—a fastening device made by peening a bulge in both ends of a metal pin.

Rockwell test—a test used to determine hardness of a sample. A machine called a Rockwell Hardness Tester drops a diamond point onto a sample at a given load and measures the depth of penetration. The disadvantage of this test for knifemakers is that it measures only hardness, not toughness or wear-resistance.

safe edge—the part of a file on which teeth have been removed. This edge will not cut and so is considered safe. The safe edge is very useful in controlling detailed file work.

sanding stick—a simple tool consisting of abrasive paper wrapped around a narrow, flat board. Sanding sticks increase leverage and control when using sandpaper.

scales—another name for slabs, the sides of a knife handle.

Scotch-Brite—the trade name for a scratchy plastic material used to make scouring pads. These pads are handy for cleaning oxidized metal. They also create an attractive frosted finish.

self-handled knife—a knife in which the steel of the tang is the only handle. Throwing knives have traditionally been of this style, but recently this style has found a wider application.

silicon carbide—a very hard manmade substance used in making coated abrasives (sandpaper).

silver (hard) solder—an alloy of more than 90% silver used to join metal at temperatures over 1,300°F. This is a confusing term because there is a soft solder that contains a small amount of silver and is also called silver solder. To make matters more confusing, there is one particular alloy of silver solder called Hard solder. Other popular grades of silver solder are known as Easy and Medium.

slab – another name for scales, the flat pieces that are used for the handle of a knife.

soft solder – any of a number of alloys used to join metals. Soft solders have lead and/or tin as a principal ingredient, and melt between 400° and 600°F. A popular variation is made of 96% tin and 4% silver. This is a strong and bright-colored solder, but it is not as strong as silver (hard) solder.

spark test – a method of holding a sample of steel against a rotating grinding wheel to make sparks. To the trained eye, the size, shape, and color of the sparks indicate the alloying constituents.

spheroidizing – a metallurgical technique that uses controlled heating to convert irregularly shaped crystals in steel into ball-shaped particles.

spring – the part of a folding knife that causes the blade to snap open and closed and to stay in its handle until opened. It is usually made of a spring steel with between 0.75% and 1% carbon.

spine – the thickest section of a blade.

stag – another name for deer antler.

stock removal – a general term for the process of shaping knives by selective grinding/ filing away of material. It is an alternate method to forging.

strop – to burnish a sharpened edge by stroking it forcibly against a flexible material like leather or canvas. The term also refers to the strap used. It can be used plain but is more often treated with a mild abrasive like rouge.

Swiss pattern files – a broad term that describes a higher grade of file, modeled in shape and cut after European files.

tang – that part of a knife that is not the blade.

tap – the tool used to cut threads inside a hole. Also the process of cutting threads.

temper – to relieve stresses in hardened steel without greatly diminishing the toughness and wear resistance of steel.

threading die – the die used to cut external threads on a rod.

through-tang – a knife configuration in which a narrow tang extends through the handle.

toughness – the ability of a metal to resist breaking.

tripoli – a fine abrasive compound made of sandstone. It is used to remove small scratches from metal and is associated with machine buffing.

water stone – a soft sandstone used to sharpen blades. It is not only used wet but also must be kept submerged for storage.

wear resistance – the ability of a metal to resist abrasion.

welt – the thick leather piece used to enlarge a sheath.

white diamond – a commercial compound similar to tripoli. It is used to remove small scratches but is faster-cutting and leaves a brighter polish than tripoli. Despite the name, it contains no diamond.

wrought iron – an alloy of iron with less than 0.2% carbon and few impurities. It is known for its ease in welding and its great malleability. Wrought iron is no longer commercially available, but ingenious blacksmiths scavenge it from antique railings and wagon wheels.

Appendix

Table 1
HEALTH HAZARDS AND SHOP SAFETY

Your best friend for safety advice is your common sense. Read these warnings and follow them, but don't rely on magic to see that the information given here finds its way into your day-to-day work. Think about what you are doing, consider the effects, and only then, begin to work. The following list describes some common materials and gives summary information. It is *not comprehensive* and should be augmented by detailed information from periodicals and books exclusively on this subject.

Compound	Effects	Precautions
Acetone	Headaches, drowsiness	Ventilation
Acetylene	Intoxicant (small doses) Cuts off oxygen (large doses)	Ventilation Check equipment regularly
Alcohol (all kinds)	Intoxication, blindness, damage to nervous system	Ventilation
Ammonia	Irritant to eyes, caustic to lungs	Use diluted, with ventilation
Aqua regia	Strongest of all acids	VENTILATION
Asbestos	Carcinogen; can take 20 years to show effects	Avoid it
Asphaltum	Toxic by skin contact; avoid inhalation and ingestion	Ventilation, wear protective gloves

Benzene (Benzol)	Intoxication, respiratory failure, coma	Avoid it
Buffing Compounds	Eye irritation, respiratory problems (i.e. shortness of breath)	Wear a respirator and goggles
Coal	Dust and fumes are toxic	Ventilation
Hydrochloric Acid	Corrosive to skin, fumes are harmful to eyes and lungs	Ventilation; wear gloves/respirator
Ketones (solvent in thinners of all kinds)	Skin, eye, nose, and throat irritants; causes nausea, vomiting, unconsciousness	Ventilation, wear protective gloves
Nickel	Fumes can cause skin allergy and eye irritation	Ventilation; wear a respirator
Nitric Acid	Corrosive to skin; fumes are harmful to eyes and lungs	Ventilation; wear a respirator
Sulfuric Acid	Corrosive to skin; fumes are harmful to eyes and lungs	Ventilation; wear a respirator

Remember, this list can't include all the materials in your shop. Read manufacturer's labels, and consult a doctor if you have any unexplained symptoms.

Table 2
SOME POPULAR TOOL STEELS

% of elements

Type	Carbon	Manganese	Silicon	Chromium	Nickel	Vanadium	Tungsten	Molybdenum
W2	0.6–1.4					0.25		
W3	1.00					0.50		
W4	0.6–1.4				0.25			
S1	0.50			1.50			2.50	
S2	0.50		1.00					0.50
S3	0.50			0.75			1.00	
01	0.90	1.00		0.50			0.50	
02	0.90	1.60						
06	1.45	1.00	1.25					0.25
A2	1.00	0.60		5.25		0.25		1.00
A4	1.00	2.00		1.00				1.00
D1	1.00			12.00				1.00
D2	1.50			12.00				1.00
D3	2.25			12.00				
L1	1.00		1.25					
L2	0.5–1.10		1.00			0.20		
L6	0.70			0.75	1.50			0.25
L7	1.00	0.35		1.40				0.40
440C	0.95–1.20	1.00	1.00	16.00–18.00				0.75
154CM	1.05	0.60	0.25	14.00				4.00

Table 3
STEEL CLASSIFICATION

The chart of popular steels in chapter 2 is reprinted here for easy reference. It uses categories of steel indicated by a single letter followed by a one- or two-digit number. An alternate classification method, based on chemical composition, is described below.

This method uses 4- or 5-digit numbers. The first number is a code: 1 indicates a carbon steel; 2, a nickel steel; 3, a nickel chromium steel, and so on. In the case of simple alloys, the second digit indicates the approximate percentage of the principal alloying element. The last 2 or 3 digits indicate the mean carbon content, in hundredths of a percent.

An example: the number *1095* signifies a carbon steel (1), with no other important alloying element (0). This steel contains about 0.95% carbon. Another example: *2520* represents a nickel steel with about 5% nickel and 0.20% carbon.

10xx	Carbon steels
11xx	Carbon steels with high sulfur, low phosphorus
12xx	Carbon steels with high sulfur, high phosphorus
23xx	Manganese 1.60 to 1.90%
25xx	Nickel 5.00%
31xx	Nickel 1.25%, chromium 0.60%
32xx	Nickel 1.75%, chromium 1.00%
33xx	Nickel 3.50%, chromium 1.50%
40xx	Molybdenum 0.25%
41xx	Chromium 1.00%, molybdenum 0.20%
43xx	Nickel-chromium-molybdenum
46xx	Nickel 1.75%, molybdenum 0.25%
48xx	Nickel 3.50%, molybdenum 0.25%
51xx	Chromium 0.80%
52xx	Chromium 1.50%
61xx	Chromium-vanadium
86xx	Nickel 0.555%, chromium 0.50%, molybdenum 0.25%
92xx	Manganese 0.80%, silicon 2.00%
93xx	Nickel 3.25%, chromium 1.20%, molybdenum 0.12%
98xx	Nickel 1.00%, chromium 0.80%, molybdenum 0.25%

Table 4
SOME COMMON NONFERROUS METALS

Symbol	Material	Make-up	Melting Point °C	°F	Specific Gravity
A1	Aluminum	element	660	1,220	2.7
Sb	Antimony	element	631	1,168	6.6
Bi	Bismuth	element	271	520	9.8
260	Brass (Cartridge)	70% Cu, 30% Zn	954	1,749	8.5
226	Brass (Nu-Gold)	88% Cu, 12% Zn	1,030	1,886	8.7
220	Brass (Red)	90% Cu, 10% Zn	1,044	1,910	8.8
511	Bronze	96% Cu, 4% Zn	1,060	1,945	8.8
Cr	Chromium	element	1,890	3,434	6.9
Cu	Copper	element	1,083	1,981	8.9
Fe	Iron	element	1,535	2,793	7.9
Pb	Lead	element	327	621	11.3
Mg	Magnesium	element	651	1,204	1.7
	Monel Metal	60% Ni, 33% Cu, 7% Fe	1,360	2,480	8.9
Ni	Nickel	element	1,455	2,651	8.8
725	Nickel (German) Silver	65% Cu, 18% Ni, 17% Zn	1,110	2,030	8.8
	Carbon Steel	99% Fe, 1% C	1,511	2,750	7.9
	Stainless Steel	91% Fe, 9% Cr	1,371	2,500	7.8
Zn	Zinc	element	419	786	7.1

Table 5
MOH'S SCALE

A loosely arranged system of relative hardness. A sample will scratch all materials with a lower number, and can be scratched by all materials with a higher number. The first line shows the original Moh's Scale, intended for use in identifying minerals. The other columns place some familiar materials along the chart.

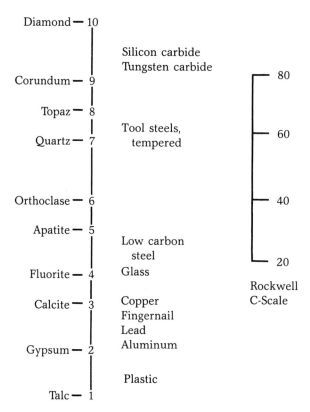

Table 6
COMPARATIVE MEASURES

1 meter	=	100 centimeters	=	3.28 feet	=	29.37 inches
1 foot	=	12 inches	=	30.48 centimeters	=	.3333 yards
1 inch	=	25.4 millimeters	=	2.54 centimeters	=	.0277 yards
1 gallon	=	4 quarts	=	8 pints	=	3.785 liters
1 US fluid oz.	=	29.57 cubic cm.	=	1.8 cubic inches	=	.0295 liter
1 lb. troy	=	12 oz. troy	=	13.165 oz. avoir.	=	5,760 grains
1 lb. avoir.	=	16 oz. avoir.	=	14.58 oz. troy	=	7,000 grains
1 kilogram	=	2.2 lb. avoir.	=	2.67 lb. troy	=	35.274 oz. avoir.
1 oz. avoir.	=	18.229 dwt.	=	.9114 oz. troy	=	28.35 grams
1 oz. troy	=	20 dwt.	=	1.097 oz. avoir.	=	31.103 grams

avoir. = avoirdupois   dwt. = pennyweight

Table 7
COMPARATIVE SIZES (approximate*)

Millimeters	Inches	B & S Gauge	Drill Size
6.50	0.257	2	–
6.25	0.246	–	–
6.00	0.236	–	–
5.75	0.226	3	1
5.50	0.217	–	–
5.25	0.207	–	–
5.00	0.197	–	8
4.75	0.187	–	–
4.50	0.177	5	15
4.25	0.167	–	–
4.00	0.157	–	22
3.75	0.148	–	26
3.50	0.138	–	29
3.25	0.128	8	30
3.00	0.118	–	31
2.75	0.108	–	–
2.50	0.098	–	40
2.25	0.088	11	43
2.00	0.078	12	47
1.75	0.068	–	50
1.50	0.059	–	53
1.25	0.049	16	56
1.00	0.039	18	60
0.75	0.030	–	69
0.50	0.020	24	76
0.25	0.010	29	80

*These numbers have been rounded to make comparisons easier.

Table 8
TEMPERATURE CONVERSION

To convert centigrade to Fahrenheit:
    –Multiply the degrees centigrade by 9,
    –Divide by 5,
    –Add 32.
To convert Fahrenheit to centigrade:
    –Subtract 32 from the degrees Fahrenheit,
    –Multiply by 5,
    –Divide by 9.

C	F	C	F	F	C	F	C
0	32	650	1,202	32	0	1,300	704
50	122	675	1,247	100	38	1,350	732
75	167	700	1,292	150	66	1,400	760
100	212	725	1,337	200	93	1,450	788
125	257	750	1,382	250	121	1,500	816
150	302	775	1,427	300	149	1,550	843
175	347	800	1,472	350	177	1,600	871
200	392	825	1,517	400	204	1,650	899
225	437	850	1,562	450	232	1,700	927
250	482	875	1,607	500	260	1,750	954
275	527	900	1,652	550	288	1,800	982
300	572	925	1,697	600	316	1,850	1,010
325	617	950	1,742	650	343	1,900	1,038
350	662	975	1,787	700	371	1,950	1,066
375	707	1,000	1,832	750	399	2,000	1,093
400	752	1,025	1,877	800	427	2,050	1,121
425	797	1,050	1,922	850	454	2,100	1,149
450	842	1,075	1,967	900	482	2,150	1,177
475	887	1,100	2,012	950	510	2,200	1,204
500	932	1,125	2,057	1,000	538	2,250	1,232
525	977	1,150	2,102	1,050	566	2,300	1,260
550	1,022	1,175	2,147	1,100	593	2,350	1,288
575	1,067	1,200	2,192	1,150	621	2,400	1,316
600	1,112	1,225	2,237	1,200	649	2,450	1,343
625	1,157	1,250	2,282	1,250	677	2,500	1,371

Suppliers

Every effort has been made to offer an up-to-date listing. In addition to these companies, you should consult a regional commercial directory and the local Yellow Pages. Many suppliers send representatives to knife shows, and of course any contact with fellow knifemakers is likely to yield valuable sources.

Some suppliers require a payment of a dollar or two for their catalog to defray publishing and mailing costs. This is usually applied to the first purchase. Some of the suppliers listed offer toll-free telephone service. Most request that you use this number only for ordering.

1 – blade steel   5 – power equipment
2 – precut blades   6 – hand tools
3 – knife findings   7 – jewelrymaking supplies
4 – handle materials

	1	2	3	4	5	6	7
Allcraft Supply 100 Frank Road Hicksville, NY 11801 (800) 645-7124 (516) 433-1660			•		•	•	•
Anchor Tool Box 265 Chatham, NJ 07928 (201) 635-2094	•			•		•	•

Anderson Cutlery & Supply
Box 383
Newtown, CT 06470
(203) 426-8623   •

Atlanta Cutlery
Box 839
Conyers, GA 30207
(404) 922-3700   •   •   •

Holt-Sornberger Supply
1253 Birchwood Drive
Sunnyvale, CA 94086
(408) 745-0306   •   •   •   •   •

Knife & Gun Finishing Supplies
Box 13522
Arlington, TX 76013
(817) 274-1282   •   •   •   •   •   •

Koval Knives
Box 14130
Columbus, OH 43214
(614) 888-6486   •   •   •   •   •   •

Bob Scrimsher's
Custom Knifemaker's Supply
Box 308
Emory, TX 75440
(214) 328-2453   •   •   •   •   •   •

Sheffield Knifemakers Supply
Box 141
Deland, FL 32720
(904) 734-7884   •   •   •   •

Rio Grande Supply
6901 Washington, N.E.
Albuquerque, NM 87109
(800) 545-6566
(505) 345-8511   •   •   •

Miscellaneous:
Blacksmithing Equipment
  Centaur Forge Ltd.
  Box 239
  Burlington, WI 53105
  (414) 763-9175

Ivory:
  Purdy's, Inc.
  2505 Cantabery
  Hays, KS 67601
  (913) 625-7676

Bibliography

BOOKS

Andrews, Jack. *Edge of the Anvil*. Emmaus, Pa.: Rodale Press, 1977.

Avner, Sidney H. *Introduction to Physical Metallurgy*. New York: McGraw-Hill Book Company, 1964

Barney, Richard W., and Loveless, Robert W. *How to Make Knives*. North Hollywood, Cal.: Beinfeld Publishing, 1977.

Boye, David. *Step-By-Step Knifemaking*. Emmaus, Pa.: Rodale Press, 1977.

*Evans, Chuck. *Jewelry, Contemporary Design and Technique*. Worcester, Mass.: Davis Publications, 1983.

Mayes, Jim. *How to Make Your Own Knives*. New York: Everest House Publishers, 1978.

*McCreight, Tim. *Metalworking for Jewelry*. New York: Van Nostrand Reinhold, 1979.

————. *The Complete Metalsmith*. Worcester, Mass.: Davis Publications, 1982.

Meilach, Dona Z. *Decorative and Sculptural Ironwork*. New York: Crown Publishers, 1977.

Smith, Cyril Stanley. *A Search for Structure*. Cambridge, Mass.: The MIT Press, 1981.

Untracht, Oppi. *Metal Techniques for Craftsmen*. New York: Doubleday and Company, 1968.

*Von Neumann, Robert. *The Design and Creation of Jewelry*. Radnor, Pa.: Chilton Publishing Company, 1961, rev. 1972.

Warner, Ken, ed. *Knives '83*. Northfield. Ill.: DBI Books, Inc., 1982.

Weygers, Alexander. *The Making of Tools*. New York, Van Nostrand Reinhold, 1973.

————

*Jewelrymaking texts.

PERIODICALS

The Anvil's Ring (quarterly). The official publication of the Artist-Blacksmiths' Association of North America (ABANA), P.O. Box 1191, Gainesville, FL 32602.

The Blade Magazine (bimonthly), 2835 Hickory Valley Road, Chattanooga, TN 37421.

Edges (quarterly). Published for the members of the American Blade Collectors by American Blade, Inc., P.O. Box 22007, Chattanooga, TN 37422.

Knife World (monthly), P.O. Box 3395, Knoxville, TN 37927.

Metalsmith (quarterly). The official publication of the Society of North American Goldsmiths (SNAG), 6707 North Santa Monica Blvd., Milwaukee, WI 53217.

Index

1-800-292-0660

79 95 + S H

00 dp to
Jewel freak

6960 East gll Blw

Lebanon TN 37090

_____

1-800- 241-3000

Mony mily Sent   9 35 - 39 90

39 95   mily mn
         po Box 3215z

phonix AZ 85069